STORIES
&
LESSONS

FROM REGIS PROGRAIS

THE FIRST 2X WORLD BOXING CHAMPION
IN NEW ORLEANS HISTORY

AS TOLD TO: ROSS WILLIAMS

Published by Williams Commerce

First Printing, 2024

ISBN: 979-8-9895223-0-9

Author

IG: @regisprograis

X: @RPrograis

YouTube: @RougaLyfeTV

Co-Author

IG & X: @rwcommercellc

Publisher

IG | FB | X: @wcwriting1

Visit Our Website

Williamscommerce1.com

Williams Commerce, LLC

Table of Contents

To understand an adult,
you must learn about their
childhood and upbringing.

———————

LESSON

CHAPTER 1

It's Deeper Than Me

I f you've ever heard the name Regis Prograis, one of the first things that probably come to mind is boxing, a loving father and husband, or a loyal friend. When my paternal family heard the name Regis Prograis before 1989, they thought of someone other than myself. They thought of my uncle.

My Uncle Regis was born on October 23, 1964, in Detroit, Michigan, six years after my father, Vidal Prograis, and one year before their brother Raynard. I always admired my dad's mental strength, but I grasped a deeper understanding of it once I dug deeper into my family history.

My paternal grandparents were a part of the Great Migration after WWII in the 1940s. Millions of African Americans fled from the South to the North in search of better lives economically and socially. My grandmother moved from Mallet, Louisiana, and my grandfather moved from New Orleans, Louisiana. They built their family in the Motor City, but not the economic prosperity they desired.

Detroit's economic decline and my dad's upbringing happened simultaneously. During my father and uncles' grade school years in the 1970s, Detroit became known as "The Murder City." The crime-ridden streets weren't at the top of the list of my father's tribulations.

My Uncle Regis added a new element of joy to the household when he was born. He spent his early childhood making people laugh and exemplifying an unlimited future. One of his childhood highlights happened when he was seven years old and stole the show at a wedding as a ring bearer. Two weeks later, he was diagnosed with leukemia.

My Uncle Regis's future appeared limitless until he started experiencing health problems. His battle with the deadly and painful disease kept him in the hospital more than at home. He became so popular that the local newspapers featured him in several articles. Each one spoke about how much joy he added to the world and other people.

His upbeat spirit gave everyone hope that he would prevail through his trial of leukemia. On December 26, 1976, a Detroit newspaper stated, "Regis, who is clearly the favorite among the nurses on Sixth Southwest, has been in the hospital for two weeks in his most recent fight with a continuing battle against leukemia."

On April 27, 1977, my uncle lost his battle with leukemia at the tender age of 12. Although he spent half of his life living in the shadow of death, he intentionally added joy to others. My Uncle Regis never stepped foot in the ring, but he was the first fighter in my family. Doctors told him he wouldn't live to see his 10th birthday. Contrary to their predictions, he died a few months before becoming a teenager.

After my uncle's death, my dad began calling out to him for comfort, guidance, and protection during his adversity-filled upbringing. My uncle's spirit lived on through my dad, and now his name lives on through me.

…

My first conscious childhood memory happened in April 1991, when my sister India was born. I don't remember taking any steps until she started following them. Many siblings develop a rivalry, but we immediately became best friends. My love for India made me a protector before my first childhood fight.

Fighting became a part of my life once I began making friendships. Cedric was my first childhood friend. We became close before grade school. He was only one year older than me, but acted like he was five years older. Our friendship was generational and developed before we were born. Our grandmothers and mothers were friends.

Cedric and I were tight from day one, but things weren't always smooth. I would grow frustrated halfway into our play sessions because he always tried to bully me. When I found out we were going to the same elementary school, I wondered how he would act with me in front of other kids.

Surprisingly, he treated me like one of his closest friends at Jean Gordon Elementary. Therefore, I became cool with most of his friends. Cedric's best friend turned one of my most embarrassing moments into an empowering one.

During a lunch period my 2nd grade year, I became the center of attention for the wrong reasons. Everyone was making fun of me, including nerds and people who barely joked around. The bombardment of jokes reduced me to tears.

While I walked out of the cafeteria with tears running down my face, Cedric's best friend put his arm around me and said, "They are just words. Don't let them bring you down."

His support meant the world to me at the time and guided my mindset about rarely taking things personally. I thought about discussing the incident with my parents that night, but the situation was already resolved. I was no longer vulnerable to words used against me.

My dad began instilling principles in me at a young age. Being reckless was second nature, but my dad's tutelage and guidance ensured certain principles weren't overstepped. One day, he caught Cedric and me bullying a kid at a school fair. The disappointment on his face made me put an end to bullying and stand up for others getting bullied.

Regardless of the innocent childhood bullying, everyone loved Cedric. He was a ladies' man, intelligent, stylish, athletic, and funny. We experienced priceless memories together in elementary school, but our deepest moments occurred later in life.

My first extracurricular activity as a child was a glimpse of my future. In second grade, my father put me in karate, but that didn't last long. I couldn't stop following through on my punches. The final straw happened once I broke another kid's jaw. Nonetheless, a seed was planted.

After getting banned from the karate studio, my father redirected me to football and basketball. I enjoyed playing in games, but practicing them didn't pique my interest. A sport can't be more than a hobby if it isn't practiced outside of practice. Throughout my childhood, I felt destined for greatness, but didn't know my path to it.

While searching for my identity at the turn of the 20th century, my city embraced a new identity. Sports and hip-hop are the soundtracks of inner-city communities in the United States. Sports are viewed as a way out, and music helps cope with inner-city life.

Before the 2000s, New Orleans was known for jazz and football. While they are at the foundation of the culture, rap music and basketball became a part of my city's identity, as well. The Charlotte Hornets moved to New Orleans in 2002 and became the city's first professional basketball team since the New Orleans Jazz in the 1970s. The NBA franchise brought a lot of buzz to the city, along with the Cash Money Millionaires and No Limit Soldiers. Both groups built musical and entertainment empires. They provided the world with snapshots of what it was like growing up in the inner city of New Orleans.

During my upbringing, a group of kids couldn't consider themselves real friends if they never pretended like they were the Hot Boys. Dank, Primo, Splash, and I pretended to be the legendary rap group. We spent almost every day growing up together, along with Brian, who was always like a little brother to me, our close friends Russ and Jacoby, and several others I remain close to until this day. Most of us saw sports or music as ways to attain a better way of life.

To understand an adult, you must learn about their childhood and upbringing. My friends and I love each other to death, but most of our fun came from insulting and fighting each other. None of us had it easy, and we needed each other's solidarity to push through our trials and tribulations. Many things we deemed normal aren't typical to the outside world.

Fighting was a method of survival in my environment growing up. Kids unable to defend themselves were constant targets at school, the playground, and my neighborhood. My light skin made me a target in the streets I grew up on, but I developed a reputation for having hands.

My dad is several shades lighter than me and has green eyes. He experienced colorism growing up in Detroit and had to prove his toughness because of his features. Knowing I would face those same obstacles, he emphasized mental strength and self-protection. Being mentally prepared to fight at a young age laid a foundation for my love of fighting. Fear prevents many from becoming their best self, but I put myself in so many dangerous situations growing up that fear empowers me.

Even though we fought each other often,
we fought others twice as hard and always
had each other's back.

_____

LESSON

CHAPTER 2

Fighting Every Step of The Way

A fight was waiting for me almost every step of the way during childhood. One brawl nearly took a turn for the worse. Three girls were walking around the corner from Kenilworth, the playground where India, my friends, and I played novice sports in the New Orleans East. Primo, Russ, and I forgot where we were headed when we saw a group of pretty girls walking on the other side of the street.

Primo crossed the street and yelled, "Oh, red skirt!"

She smacked her mouth and said, "Boy, that ain't my name!"

Primo flashed a grin he normally charmed girls with, then responded, "Well, tell me what it is then, baby."

The girl wearing the red skirt didn't smile back and said, "I have an old man, and my friends do too."

Russ and I took heed of her statement and kept walking in the other direction. Primo didn't do the same and replied, "I ain't worried about your dusty ass old man."

Then they exchanged words, and we continued in the other direction. While walking off, she made threats about what her boyfriend and his friends would do to us. We carried on with the rest of our day and quickly forgot about her threats. In less than 24 hours, we were reminded.

The next day, we crossed paths with the same girls at the same location. This time, they had company. Red Skirt's boyfriend and his friends looked too old to talk to girls our age. Age gaps during childhood and teenage years are more significant than any other age discrepancies. None of us hit puberty yet, but the guys there to fight us were fully developed men.

We knew what time of day it was when Red Skirt's boyfriend walked toward Primo and aggressively said, "Tell me what you were saying yesterday!"

Before Primo could answer, her boyfriend swung at him and missed badly. Then Primo showed me how irrelevant muscles are in a fight. Primo was outmatched physically, but he sidestepped her boyfriend and dropped him with three quick punches.

Once Primo got on top of him, one of the guy's friends jumped in. Then, one by one, we all started fighting. After I dropped the biggest guy in their group, I got dropped with a hard right. This was the first time I got hit and wasn't able to regain my footing. I landed headfirst on the curb.

The person who hit me wrapped his sweaty and massive hands around my neck, then tried squeezing the life out of it. I felt the air leaving my body like a flattening tire until Russ hit him with a punch that sounded off throughout the block.

While we brawled for our lives in front of an escalating crowd, I realized how important it is to never underestimate your opponent. The guys we fought had clear physical advantages over us, but they took us lightly and got dealt with. We bullied the bullies. Our love for fighting outweighed their ability to bully us.

Primo and I fought more than all my other friends combined. When all of us hung out, we knew it would only be a matter of time before we were wrestling or tapping out. Cell phones with cameras weren't a thing then. If they were, there would be hundreds of videos of us going at it and making our friends laugh.

His favorite place to fight me was at his grandmother's house. Primo took homecourt advantage to another level. He knew I wouldn't want to damage anything in her house. She is still one of the sweetest women I ever met.

On this particular day, Primo didn't have any interest in going outside. He was the only gamehead in my group. He could play the video game all day, but Splash, Dank, and I preferred to be outside.

We grew frustrated that he was holding us up from going outside because he wanted to finish a game of Madden. Dank whispered, "Cut the game off on that boy Regis."

This was the memory card era of video games. I knew his game wasn't saved, but I didn't care because I wanted to go outside. Daring each other to do things was a typical occurrence.

Dank and I looked at Primo hunched over and yelling at the screen, trying to mount a comeback. He scored one touchdown, but didn't get a chance to score another one because I snatched the video game plug out of the wall.

After he screamed, "Man, what the fuck Regis!" He tackled me as if he was auditioning to become a linebacker for the New Orleans Saints. Dank and I laughed hysterically while he yelled at the top of his lungs. The laughs ended once we put a hole in his grandmother's wall.

Even though we fought each other often, we fought others twice as hard and always had each other's back. One of my favorite childhood presents caused a fight. This type of gift became the reason for many violent crimes or thievery acts across the country.

In New Orleans, many kids get a taste of adulthood and have to grow up quickly. Learning what hard work was in the humid New Orleans heat gave me a taste of responsibilities during my childhood. My hustle graduated from cutting grass to contractor work with my older cousin, George. He would pick me up at 6:00 AM on weekends and drop me off at 9:00 PM. That $100 at the end of the workday felt gratifying and made me more appreciative of my parents' sacrifices to provide for India and me.

I used my hard-earned money to purchase a pair of tan and white Jordan 13s for my 12th birthday. They were special to me because I earned the money to pay for them, and I rarely wore flashy clothes as a kid. I was comfortable with clothes from Walmart as long as they matched.

I purchased them a few days before my house party, but decided not to wear them until the celebration. The front of my house and garage were popular in my neighborhood. I had a basketball goal in front of my house, and my friends and I spent a lot of time hanging out in the garage.

We had a good turnout for my birthday, and I felt loved that day for the most part. Things went left when the party was coming to an end. My friends and I put our shoes in the garage at the beginning of the party. Once it was time to put our shoes back on, my brand-new Jordans were missing.

I knew my closest friends would never do such a thing, but there were too many people outside my circle to decipher who jacked my shoes. Everyone knew I didn't lose them. My close friends felt my anger too, but there wasn't much we could do about it at the time.

A few months later, my anger resurfaced. Kerry, an acquaintance from the neighborhood, was one of the last few people I invited to the party. I regretted inviting Kerry when I caught him wearing my shoes on the other side of town.

My grandparents and I were on the way to pick up commodity food from a church. We were miles away from our neighborhood and a few months removed from the incident, but I wasn't letting it slide. It was meant for me to see him that day.

Primo was the first person I told when I returned home. Kerry always roamed the neighborhood, so we knew where to find him. We caught up with him several hours after I saw him parlaying the streets wearing my Jordans. When I called his name, he acted as if he saw a ghost.

He tried playing it off, but he was a terrible actor. Primo and I were a step ahead of him and decided to play stupid, also. A smart person can play stupid, but a stupid person can't play smart.

We acted as if everything was all good and asked him to come play basketball at my house. Although Jordans are basketball shoes, no one dared to get them scuffed up playing meaningless games in the streets. Kerry treated the shoes he stole from me with no respect, and that made me feel even more disrespected.

When we returned to my house, I said, "You know I want my round, right?"

I expected the fear on his face. Kerry always got himself in fights, but shied away from them. He didn't have a choice to leave without fighting, but I gave him an option.

Once we entered my garage, I asked, "Would you rather fight Primo or me?"

He quickly chose to fight Primo. His choice didn't improve his outcome. Primo left several lumps on his face after they scrapped.

The aftermath of that fight showed how much times have changed in society. Most people who get the worst of a street fight these days would retaliate with guns or end the relationship. After Kerry's face was lumped up, like when Tommy Hearns fought Martin Lawrence on his hit TV show, we all shook hands and continued being cool. He just wasn't invited to my house anymore.

With each level we climb to, a new set of
challenges will be waiting for us.

———————

LESSON

CHAPTER 3

The Foundation

My house and family were a sense of stability for more than my sister and me. Most of my friends grew up in broken homes, and some didn't have relationships with one or both of their parents.

My parents' relationship seemed perfect during my early years. They worked hard together to provide India and me with the best opportunities they could. We attended magnet schools outside our district, participated in extracurricular activities, and went on family vacations to Las Vegas and Detroit.

After one event during my childhood, I noticed a shift in my parents' relationship. Before then, we did everything as a unit. My dad and mom got into an argument in front of everyone, and it seemed like that incident created a wedge in their relationship.

My parents began doing their own thing and detached from one another. Their pain was too deep to conceal, along with their actions. Consequently, I inherited some of the pain they endured.

I grew accustomed to people fighting or not getting along and getting over it. My parents would have good streaks and times when they got along, and I was confident they would work it out. Their problems were no longer private, and my friends began joking about them. I joked about their family issues as well, but that was how we laughed the pain away.

My middle school years reiterated how important family and friendships are. My parents sent me to Marian Central for middle school. This was my first time attending a Catholic school.

New Orleans is a Catholic city. The Saints are our NFL mascot, Catholic schools are abundant, and Catholicism is the predominant religion. The stricter environment was an adjustment, but my friends and grandparents eased the transition.

My maternal grandparents were soulmates and epitomized real love. They loved the air each other breathed and the ground they walked on. My mother's parents did everything together, including being active grandparents. India and I walked to their house every day after elementary school.

I continued my after-school routine during middle school. The walk to my grandparents was a mile and a half longer, but nothing would stop me from ending my schooldays at their house. The love I received from my grandparents made me hurry there after school. I chose to hang out with them instead of my classmates. They treated India and me as if we were only children. When talking with them, they made it seem like nothing else in the world existed.

I was further removed from sports than ever during middle school. Basketball and flag football were my only options at school. Flag football removed the part of the game I liked the most, and we had one of the best basketball teams in the city. Therefore, I didn't participate in any school sports. I spent most of my time in middle school hanging with my friends and grandparents.

Splash was the jokester of my group. He always added laughter, whether intentionally or unintentionally. One day after school, he encouraged me to go by a girl's house who I attended Marian Central with and lived in our neighborhood. As a way of trying to get out of going, I told him he had to come with me. That plan backfired when he agreed, then rode me on his handlebars to her house.

Splash hung out on her couch while she and I chilled alone. We heard a noise outside her room, but thought it was my friend. When we heard a voice well past puberty, we scrambled to the kitchen. Initially, she told me her father wouldn't be home until three hours later, but he was less than three seconds away.

Splash pulled me into the closet. Then she ran back to her room. Her dad yelled her name, but she didn't answer. Splash and I were shoulder-to-shoulder, peeking at her dad through the cracks of the closet. It sounded like he was about to yank the closet door open at any moment.

Once she didn't answer him, her dad turned the TV on and sat down to eat. Splash and I were starving before we made it over there. Now, we were hunched in a closet, smelling Popeyes chicken on an empty stomach.

We debated what we should do under our breaths and with exaggerated hand gestures. Her dad seemed glued to the couch a few feet away from us. Right after we agreed to make a run for it, Splash passed gas. We covered our noses and tried concealing our laughs.

I was prepared to accept the consequences. I thought there was no way he didn't hear us. While Splash was still laughing, I swung the closet door open and ran for the back door without looking in her dad's direction. Splash and I ran for two blocks. Once we caught our breath, Splash said, "Thank God he was sleep!"

Marian Central had its moments, but it wasn't the middle school experience I hoped for. My father shot down my plans to attend Gregory for middle school. Cedric went there, and they had a tackle football team and the public school atmosphere I desired to be in.

I wanted to go to Sarah T. Reed for high school twice as much as I wanted to attend Gregory. Dank, Splash, and many of my friends and family in the neighborhood went there. My dad shot down those plans also and sent me to McDonough 35 for high school. He sold me on them having a decent football program and many successful alums. The magnet high school in the 7th Ward of New Orleans was another step further from my neighborhood.

My first year in high school showed me that with each level we climb to, a new set of challenges awaits us. I didn't have many challenges and obstacles during elementary and middle school, but I stepped on a landmine when I entered high school.

I learned first-hand about the importance of having
a father in the household. My father's assistance with school
kept me afloat academically, but more importantly, he helped
me develop into a man by teaching me
principles in his own way.

LESSON

CHAPTER 4

Landmine

Football was my primary sport during my freshman year in high school. My basketball career ended with AAU the summer after 8th grade. My dad and I always spent a lot of time together, but we spent more time together than ever the summer heading into high school. He was more than involved in everything India and I participated in athletically and became a coach on my AAU basketball team.

Most of my teammates were from single-parent homes, and their only parent was too busy trying to make ends meet to show up to any games. My dad went the extra mile by coaching me, attending our practices in other sports, and bringing our friends to their extra-curricular activities, even if India and I weren't involved. It didn't matter that I wasn't a standout or champion in the other sports. He supported India and I like we were champions during our novice years when most kids were only worried about refreshments at the concession stands after the game.

Football and schoolwork cut into our time together at the beginning of my 9th grade year. When it finally felt like I was getting adjusted to high school, I experienced a morning that changed my world forever.

The drive from New Orleans East to the 7th Ward is considered long to most New Orleanians, although it's only a 15-minute drive. Those 15 minutes felt everlasting when my father announced to India and me that he would be moving out and wouldn't be home when we returned from school.

Tears on the inside hurt more than visible ones. My insides trembled, and I feared each moment in front of me. I locked eyes with my father when I exited his vehicle on Kelerec Drive outside of school. Usually, I walked straight into school after he dropped me off, but I watched him drive off with a piece of my heart until his truck vanished in the distance.

Each day for the next few weeks, I hoped my dad would walk through the door again, but my hope faded away day by day until a month went by. When I realized he wasn't coming back, a seed of rage was planted in my soul.

The jokes I used to laugh at were no longer funny. The food I loved didn't taste the same, and sports weren't as enjoyable without him on the sidelines. Lectures from teachers and students' conversations sounded like backdrop noise for the rest of the year. School and football were afterthoughts while dealing with the pain from my parents' divorce. Consequently, my grades suffered, and my behavior became a problem for the first time.

How was I supposed to be a model student while dealing with drastic life changes? My mom reiterated that sentiment when she convinced the school advisory board not to kick me out after 9th grade. I didn't have the minimal requirements for re-entry my sophomore year. Although I came up short, my mother went to war for me and convinced them to let me back in for another chance.

I still wanted to go to school with my friends at Reed, but my mother's hard-fought efforts made me feel obligated to give it another try. This was another example of how she always had my back.

The days of family trips to Detroit and watching scary movies as a unit while my dad conjured up creative ways to scare us felt far removed. I thought we were just going through some bumps in the road, but suddenly the road ended.

Soon after his departure, I learned first-hand about the importance of having a father in the household. My father's assistance with school kept me afloat academically, but more importantly, he helped me develop into a man by teaching me principles in his unique way.

A paintball gun my mother purchased for me was one of my favorite childhood gifts. When I first got it, I tested it on trees and abandoned houses. One day, while bored, I decided to test it on my sister. I shot it at her legs and playfully pissed her off as I often did. My dad was the first person to see what I did.

He snatched the paintball gun out of my hand and fired it at me while I ran down the street.

A normal parent's reaction during that era would have been to whip my ass with a belt, but that wasn't my father's style. When I did wrong, he did things to challenge my mind and make me think. Many adults have difficulty getting through to kids when they mess up. My dad was a master at knowing how to challenge me mentally and getting through to me. That's part of why chess was always my family's favorite game to play. I wished for more days of us playing games together, but I knew they were a part of the past.

My heart was broken when I fell
in love with boxing, but
the sport mended it.

———————

LESSON

CHAPTER 5

Blessing In Disguise

I was motivated during the first few days of my sophomore year, but quickly reverted to some old habits from my freshman year. Football seemed at a standstill, but I was thankful for the outlet.

Cedric and I were on an organized sports team together for the first time in high school. Our most meaningful interaction happened during my 10th grade year. While casually passing the locker room during my off period, I heard familiar rumblings behind the closed doors. The familiar sounds made me curious, so I knocked for verification.

One of my teammates opened the door and acted as if he was in the Secret Service. He whispered to my friends and me that if we wanted to get inside, we would have to get in the boxing gloves and fight someone. The classmates I was with walked off quickly, but I eagerly entered.

As I crossed the threshold, two of my teammates were recklessly swinging at each other. The people in the locker room were entertained, but I felt like they hadn't seen anything yet. Once they finished scrapping, one of the assistant football coaches asked, "Who's next?"

A starting linebacker took a pair of gloves out of the coach's hands, and everyone else in the room shied away from the challenge. Cedric walked toward me and confidently told the locker room, "My boy Regis will fight him."

Everyone in there doubted me except for Cedric. The coach asked if I was sure I wanted to fight one of the biggest people on the team, and I nodded without saying a word. When I slipped on the gloves, adrenaline rushed through my veins. My teammate mumbled trash talk under his breath, but he didn't know I had already knocked out people twice his size.

After we put our hands up, he tried taking my head off with his first three swings. Before he could throw his fourth punch, he ate two vicious hooks that caught him and the rest of the room off guard. The sounds of flush punches shifted the energy in the room.

The face the linebacker made after I laid hands on him is the same one I look for in every opponent I fight. His face signified a pain he couldn't overcome. Once he gave up, the room went crazy, but all I saw was Cedric nodding at me.

The look in his eyes was clearer than words. Cedric affirmed that I found my calling and was transitioning from a boy to a man. He saw me as a boxer before the world did. That look created a shift in how I saw myself.

Apparently, Cedric and I weren't the only people who saw where my future was headed during my past. I hit the peak of my football career when I started boxing in the locker room. The crowd grew every time I fought. Before then, I went through the motions at practice as a backup cornerback. I moved with a different pep in my step when I knew I would be getting in the gloves after practice.

One day, after fighting in the locker room, the defensive back's coach intercepted me once I exited the door and led me to a secluded area in the hallway. For a moment, I thought I was in trouble for going so hard on my teammate. Once we were alone, the coach, who I will forever be thankful for, asked me to turn my equipment in and pursue boxing.

Most amateur athletes would feel deterred if their coach redirected them to another sport. However, it didn't take me long to recognize the blessing in disguise. Twenty-four hours later, I entered a boxing gym for the first time. I was green about what I was getting myself into, but I knew my mind and body were in the right place.

My first visit to the boxing gym eternally anchored my heart in the ring. My heart was broken when I fell in love with boxing, but the sport mended it. When family secrets are revealed, they hurt worse than if we knew the truth from the jump. I thought the pain from my parents' fallout was healing until the family drama led me to find out my mother was adopted.

The news caught me off guard, but it didn't hurt me as much as the divorce. I was at a loss for words because of the timing I found out. Why did I have to find that out during one of the most painful times of my life? Life was testing me from every angle.

Finding out something my mother kept to herself made us closer. I developed a deeper understanding of her journey, and we were able to be there for each other in a deeper manner. The most hurtful things must be revealed to heal. Coping with pain was a lonely process, but there are blessings in every triumph. Boxing became an outlet during one of the toughest stages of my life.

New Orleans was the murder capital of the United States in 2004, and the unfortunate trend continued in 2005. There were frightful reminders on the news almost every day about the danger in our community. Nonetheless, many of my peers had already turned to a life of crime and were in the streets during our teenage years.

Going to the boxing gym limited my time around those traveling down the wrong road. When I did get free time, I divided it between my sister, close friends, family, and television. School wasn't a significant part of that equation. Consequently, my mother taught me one of my most valuable lessons.

I wasn't responsible for myself yet, so my mother was the one who set my priorities. School was a priority to her, but not to me. My mom created distance between my first love and I when she received my third quarter report card sophomore year. She wanted me to show the same passion for school that I showed for boxing. It was an unrealistic expectation, but I increased my effort enough to get back in the ring.

In retrospect, I would have achieved a 4.0 GPA if that's what it took to start boxing again. I improved my effort enough to get off punishment, but it wasn't enough to be welcomed back at my high school for junior year.

God's plans will always
override our own.

———————

LESSON

CHAPTER 6

My First Start In Boxing

The summer of 2005 was one of my first joyous times since my parents' divorce. I was headed to the high school I wanted to attend in the fall, and this would be my first summer focusing on boxing.

My starting point in boxing was my first obstacle in the sport. There were no breeding grounds for amateur boxers in New Orleans. Although my resources to develop were limited, I made the most of my surroundings.

A friend from my neighborhood unknowingly shifted my priorities at the end of my 10th grade year. He recommended me to Big Bear Boxing Club and began bragging about a boxer named Red.

I hadn't heard of Red until that interaction. The way my friend bragged about him made me want to be seen in the same light and test my skills against him. I assumed no one in New Orleans could beat me.

Big Bear was located in the Lower 9th Ward. The area known to locals as The Lower Nine, is historically known as one of the city's most crime-ridden and drug-infested areas. This was a different environment from the first gym I attended.

Coach Harry was my first mentor in boxing. He lived in the community decades before my existence and grew frustrated with the excessive crime and juvenile delinquency. Instead of complaining about it, as most people do about their problems, he made a difference by setting up a boxing ring in the empty lot next to his house. He was so influential in the community that even kids with no interest in boxing spent time there. I differentiated myself in his eyes by spending countless hours working at the sport we mutually loved during the summer of 2005.

A common misconception in society is that we can only learn from experts. Everyone on this earth knows something we don't know. Coach Harry didn't start his gym to produce world champions, but that was part of what made his gym extraordinary and unique. He was there because he genuinely cared about everyone who stepped into his ring. Many people are only in it for themselves. Coach Harry was the perfect mentor at the time and taught me a fundamental aspect of my game.

Head movement was the main thing he preached to me. Coach Harry said my head should move like the double-end bag. His advice stuck with me throughout my career. I hadn't learned the fundamentals of boxing yet, but I was a natural in the environment meant for me.

Once I connected with Coach Harry, Big Bear Boxing Club became my priority. After my first session at his house, we talked for hours as if we had a long, pre-existing relationship. That became a routine for us after we finished training.

I didn't wait long before getting in the ring with Red. He gave me my first lesson in boxing and showed me that there are levels to the sport. When I got in the ring, I tried fighting like I did in the streets. Red boxed circles around me, and I couldn't touch him. Not knowing the fundamentals made me want to learn all I could.

I trained with Red and Coach Harry as much as possible. They were the only two consistent people at the gym. Red was naturally talented, but stood out the most because of his discipline. On our third week of working out together, he asked me to take a jog with him.

He caught me off guard by saying he wanted to jog the entire Lower 9th Ward, but I was willing to go the extra mile to improve and be seen in the same light as him. I didn't say a word during the first few miles. We jogged past drug deals, crack houses, street fights, crime scenes, and other dangerous distractions.

On our third mile, a group of gorgeous girls showing off every inch of their bodies in the summer sun tried getting our attention. We caught their eyes as soon as we entered the block. I glanced at Red, and he acted as if he didn't see them. I followed suit. Once we were out of hearing distance from the girls, he said, "Man, the last person I ran with ditched me as soon as he saw some girls."

Prioritizing boxing at that moment pushed me to a new level. Within a few weeks, I surpassed most others at the gym because boxing wasn't their priority. Red was there every week, so I went every day possible to differentiate myself and catch up to him and others on a higher level.

As the summer ended, I began preparing for my first amateur bout. I couldn't wait to show my family and friends what I had been working on. Hustling to get a crowd at my first amateur fight was no easy task. I gathered a decent crowd, but the most important thing was missing - an opponent.

I grew antsy walking around the gym while my family and friends anxiously waited to see a boxing match. As my hopes dwindled, a sparring partner named Donald felt sorry for me and volunteered to fight me. All my butterflies flew away once he gave me an opportunity I'll forever be thankful for.

I gave my family and friends a glimpse of my potential by convincingly outclassing Donald. While leaving the gym that night, I felt that I officially found my lane and began walking into my calling. The support I received from my loved ones at my first amateur fight laid the foundation for continuously striving to make them proud. They cheered me on as if I won a world title.

My second amateur fight was in Biloxi, Mississippi, the weekend before my junior year. Fighting outside New Orleans for the first time exposed me to the upward mobility in boxing. I knew I was only fighting in my neighboring state, but I dreamed about fighting across the entire world. Fighting in another state heightened my focus and aspirations.

My opponent was 15 pounds heavier than me and more experienced. He used that to his advantage and pulled out a debatable victory. Spectators and I thought I won, but his hometown judges thought otherwise. While traveling back to New Orleans, I vowed to do my best to leave my fights out of the judges' hands. My maturation process began evolving when I turned that L into a lesson.

The following week, I transferred to Sarah T. Reed High School. Reed ranked at the bottom in every metric of the city's public school system. I quickly understood what my parents tried to keep me away from during the first week at my new school.

Students had sex in the bathrooms as if they were at a motel. Dice games were played as if we were at a casino. Whispered about killers and criminals attended the school, and fights were bound to occur at any moment. Nonetheless, I enjoyed every minute of my first few days.

The chaos made me forget what I was there for, but I was thrilled about finishing my high school years with my closest friends and family. I had been dreaming of this for more than a decade. One week later, I learned that God's plans will always override our own.

Pain hits differently when it is experienced collectively. Everyone from my city could identify with the permanent scars on our hearts from Hurricane Katrina.

———————

LESSON

CHAPTER 7

God's Plan

S everal cultural events sparked a unique vibe in New Orleans during the fall of 2005. The excitement transitioned to concern once the mayor issued a mandatory evacuation due to a hurricane brewing in the Gulf of Mexico.

The previous Christmas, New Orleans experienced snow for the first time in a half-century. Weather catastrophes and abnormalities were a topic worldwide, but the unthinkable was on the horizon.

In New Orleans, there are six seasons: fall, winter, spring, summer, crawfish season, and hurricane season. From the beginning of June until the end of November, New Orleans and other areas along the Gulf Coast prepare for hurricane season. My family did the typical hurricane protocols, such as boarding our windows, placing sandbags by the doors, and filling the car with gas. However, hurricane evacuations meant the same thing as a weekend getaway for me and most New Orleanians.

Typically, my sister and I would travel with our parents to a surrounding city outside the danger zone. Not being able to evacuate with my parents together dampened an occasion I usually anticipated.

My father moved to the state capital, Baton Rouge, which is one hour west of New Orleans. He and my mother had separate evacuation plans. Hours before the hurricane made landfall, my sister, cousin, and I piled into my grandparents' car, and we headed to Houston, Texas.

While Katrina tore through the Gulf, the meteorologists stated that it would be reminiscent of Hurricane Betsy. The hurricane in 1965 struck the Gulf Coast and caused over $1 billion worth of damage and 81 fatalities. The fear in my grandparents' eyes showed me that this trip was much deeper than just a weekend getaway. They lost everything in Hurricane Betsy, which was nicknamed Billion Dollar Betsy because of the damage it caused.

Although we were hurrying out of town, everything appeared to be moving in slow motion. While we left the neighborhood, I noticed things I never saw before, and my surroundings became engraved in my memory forever.

Violent storm surges headed to a city under sea level didn't have us feeling optimistic. No one could conceptualize the impact of the potential worst-case scenarios. At worst, I thought the city might flood, and we would return home to everyday life within a few weeks.

I was sadly mistaken. On August 29, 2005, we were glued to the news, watching the city we love get ripped apart by one of the worst natural disasters in world history. My house's positioning next to the lakefront was in prime position to receive peak damage. Confirmation that life would never be the same happened when we saw that my neighborhood looked no different from the lake next to it.

I was homeless in Houston, Texas, and a refugee in my own country. There was no time to feel sorry for myself because I was in survival mode, and others had it worse than me, even though I lost everything overnight. Some people drowned, experienced a death too gruesome for an open coffin, and others were never found.

Many survivors were stuck on roofs of flooded houses and apartment buildings. Over 25% of the city was sheltered in the Superdome without power, electricity, or functioning plumbing. The same arena where Muhammad Ali won his last fight was now used to shelter the city's residents fighting for their lives and an escape route.

Neighborhoods were war zones while the streets were ungoverned. People lurked and looted for survival or opportunist measures. Kids unable to fend for themselves were protected as babies in the wild. New Orleans citizens were living in inhumane conditions. The lack of planning and response intensified the storm's damages.

Pain hits differently when it is experienced collectively. Everyone from my city could identify with the permanent scars on our hearts from Hurricane Katrina. During one of my toughest times in life, I identified one of my greatest purposes.

One of my most meaningful tattoos is the one across my chest displaying the date of Hurricane Katrina. Representing New Orleans in the ring and displaying a date that brought us universal pain is a symbol meant to provide inspiration and strength for my city.

When I lost everything, I discovered that
my motivation and happiness didn't stem
from things money could buy.

———————

LESSON

CHAPTER 8

Change of Environment

Having nothing helped me find everything. The pain from a tragedy nearly two decades ago still feels fresh today. It took us a few weeks to reconnect with my parents and several months to determine who was dead or alive. Hurricane Katrina claimed more than 1800 lives, caused over $100 billion in property damage, and was the costliest natural disaster in U.S. history.

Traumatic stories were abundant. My grandparents' tears intensified the reality of the tragedy. Experiencing the hurricane at a different stage in life from them gave me a different perspective. Everything they worked decades for was destroyed overnight. They were reliving a nightmare they previously overcame.

Although all my belongings were snatched from me in the blink of an eye, I gained insight into one of the most intricate aspects of life. No matter our status or stage of life, God has the power to make us start over with nothing or end our time at any moment.

In an economy based on capitalism, material possessions have become a common motivating factor for most people. Monetary desires often influence people's career choices. When I lost everything, I discovered that my motivation and happiness didn't stem from things money could buy. I missed my friends and city more than I missed my belongings.

Being rich was a lifestyle I always desired as a kid, but I saw the value in financial freedom during the aftermath of Hurricane Katrina. A family's economic status played a major factor in determining how quickly families could recover. Financially affluent families had an easier time relocating and creating new opportunities. I was forced into early adulthood with a bitter ending to my childhood.

The expectation for India and me to continue school so soon after the traumatic experience felt unrealistic. I learned that life goes on no matter what happens to us. The rest of the country was able to carry on with everyday life, while New Orleanians had to scramble to pick up the pieces and recover from a tragedy.

I attended several different high schools during my junior year. Alief Hastings High in Houston was the first high school I attended after the hurricane. I never imagined going to high school outside of New Orleans.

Unforeseen circumstances in a new environment gave me a culture shock. Houston's academics were more advanced, and the culture was different. The high schools I attended in New Orleans were predominantly Black and had rundown facilities. Alief Hastings High could've easily been mistaken for a community college and was the most diverse setting I experienced at that point in my life.

With so many revolving doors and so much uncertainty looming, I had a feeling I wouldn't be there long. It didn't matter if I evacuated to a mansion overlooking the ocean in California. No place other than home would have been able to make me feel comfortable and ease the pain I was experiencing at the time.

New Orleans re-opened its city limits five weeks after the storm tore the city apart. Going back home to a desolate city where many lives were lost felt like a scary movie being played out in real time.

The energy that attracts millions of travelers worldwide each month didn't exist. The city where residents prowled the streets, hugged the porches throughout the day, and partied until daybreak was now desolate and patrolled by the National Guard. A trip to New Orleans for the casual visitor seemed far away. Many businesses, universities, and families had to make path-changing decisions.

Hurricane Katrina caused a new migration in U.S. history. Thousands of New Orleanians were dispersed in droves throughout the country in pursuit of a better life. The tragedy led many residents to other cities where they found opportunities that were unavailable back home. Surrounding major cities in the Bible Belt, such as Houston, Dallas, and Atlanta, received most of the evacuees. I jumped at the first opportunity to get close to home.

One of my cousins in Slidell, Louisiana, extended my grandparents, India, and me an invitation to move in with them. Eight people were living in a 3-bedroom house. My grandparents and India had a room. I slept on the floor, but I was thankful to be there. This was much better than living in a garage like we did for a few weeks in Houston. Waking up in a garage is a feeling I'll never forget.

Another reason I moved to Slidell was to attend school with Primo. He transferred to Slidell High before the storm and had already made himself at home in the suburbs. Although Slidell is on the outskirts of New Orleans, I still had wild moments there. The last time I was there before the storm, I fought a man twice my age.

Primo and I would have gotten in trouble anywhere together at that age. Trouble started with one of the last people I expected. Tim, Primo's mom's boyfriend at the time, acted as if he was our age, but he was old enough to be our father. Tim and Primo didn't get along, so he was already on bad terms with me.

One day, we were playing basketball at Primo's house in Slidell, and Tim's trash talk became personal. At one point, another adult asked him why he was talking to kids like that. We were there for a party, but nothing joyous was taking place outside. Another grown man checking Tim about disrespecting and bullying kids didn't influence him to stop.

Tim kept picking at Primo and me. He was 6 foot 6 and we were teenagers still going through puberty. Nonetheless, he still acted as if he wanted to fight us.

After we finished playing ball, I walked past him with a Nerf gun and said I should shoot one of these darts at you. He snapped back, "I wish the fuck you would!"

A dart landed on his forehead before he finished making another threat. I took off running, but stopped in my tracks and put my hands up once Primo told me to stop running. After a few traded blows, we were tumbling in a ditch.

Once I made the grown man look like a little boy, Primo began fighting him also. The fight was over once I left a knot the size of a strawberry on his head. He held an icepack on it for the rest of the party.

...

Going to school with Primo was a bright moment during a dark time. The dynamics of Slidell High shifted after the storm. Many schools that accepted a high volume of New Orleans students experienced an increase in fights and a shift in school culture.

The environment had little to do with the chaos. Many people like me evacuated with only an outfit or two and lost their way of life, irreplaceable possessions, and our city and community. It was impossible for others to understand what we were experiencing at the time.

Being pulled from one environment unexpectedly and expected to function as if everything were normal was unrealistic. My age group arguably had it the toughest out of all Katrina survivors. We weren't emotionally mature or experienced enough to deal with the adversity-filled era that was supposed to be the "best times" of our lives.

My city is known for being unique, and Hurricane Katrina added to that distinction. New Orleans people have some of the most distinct identifiers. The accent usually gives it away. If they don't proudly tell you where they are from, you will know by a fleur de lis symbol, apparel, or verbal reminder. Being unexpectedly ripped away from that culture would make the happiest person depressed.

One of the most painful things about the hurricane was its effect on my grandmother. She cried almost every day after Hurricane Katrina. The storm's aftermath showed me that there is nothing like being in your own home. If there isn't peace at home, life can feel like it's caving in.

My sister was making a smooth transition to Slidell. She joined the basketball team and quickly made friends. Slidell High was less intense than Reed, but less strict than the school I attended in Houston. Primo and I were side by side almost every moment until lunch break on my fourth day. Without him around on the basketball court, someone else tried controlling things.

Me and a group of other juniors and seniors were playing basketball at the gym. I didn't know anyone on the court, so I wasn't sure if I would be picked to play on a team for the first game.

One of the guys on the court passed me the ball and said, "You and I can pick teams."

A guy named Travis intercepted the ball and said, "Nah, fuck that. I'm picking teams with you."

He took my guaranteed spot and talked to me in a manner I didn't appreciate, but I grinned and let him pick teams. He glanced at me from the corner of his eyes before announcing his first three picks, then picked someone else. The other guy quickly selected me with his fourth pick, and Travis said, "I'm surprised you didn't have to wait until the second game. I am going to lock you up."

Travis was the tallest person on the court, but I made him feel like a little boy on the first few possessions. When he tried driving to the goal on me, I blocked his shot, and he began crying that I fouled him. He grew even more irate when other people told him it was all ball. When the same result happened on the next drive, he mouthed off, "Foul me again and watch what happens!"

The gym was packed with most of the school as if we were at a homecoming pep rally. His remarks caught several onlookers' attention. A dunk by someone else on the next play made even more people look at the game.

Once he had a bigger audience, he told me, "If you foul me again, we are throwing hands."

When Travis got the ball on the next possession, I let him drive past me. I had an ulterior motive. Once he left his feet to go for a layup, I gripped his ribs and shoved him to the ground.

Everyone ran toward the fight and experienced a changed perception of him. He had been all talk thus far. This was the moment I had been waiting for.

After Travis returned to his feet, he palmed my face and pushed it. Once he let go, an overhand left he didn't see coming knocked him on the gym floor. He hurried to his feet to try redeeming himself, but everyone saw the fear in his eyes. Travis asserted himself as a bully to everyone and now had the opportunity to live up to it.

When we threw our sets up, I iffed at him twice to bait him in. He fell for it and threw two missed punches. That left him open for two punches that sounded off throughout the crowded gym and caused a frenzy.

Faculty members hurried to the gym and escorted me directly to the principal's office. That fight instantly changed my social status at school. Girls were waving at me flirting while I was scolded in the office. Previously, people in Slidell primarily saw me as Primo's friend, but I stepped into my own light after that incident.

My friends always knew I could fight, but this was my first taste of popularity due to my fighting skills. Suddenly, I had plenty of friends and girls to choose from. Growing out of my comfort zone in a different environment made me love my new surroundings. Life was moving so fast, but it slowed down once I arrived at a fork in the road that almost every New Orleanian encountered during the turn of 2006.

Moving away from home during the
aftermath of Hurricane Katrina made me
realize how much I would be sacrificing
to chase my dreams. I sacrificed immediate
gratification for my long-term goals.

———————

LESSON

CHAPTER 9

Sacrifices

Remaining in Louisiana for the rest of my high school years was an option, but that path would've pulled me away from my destiny. When I started training in The Lower 9th Ward, I learned why many boxers from New Orleans didn't make it professionally. The city's most talented fighters never received the opportunity to display their talents under bright lights due to their affiliations with the streets and not being in an environment that fostered their growth.

I knew what I could do under the New Orleans city lights, but I outgrew that phase and wanted to spread my wings. I don't know what my boxing trajectory would have been if I remained in New Orleans, but I wouldn't reverse the hands of time to find out and bet against the hardest decision I ever made.

I decided to move to Houston with my mom instead of remaining in Slidell or returning to New Orleans. I became comfortable in Slidell. I was going to school with one of my best friends, had a good-paying job, and adapted quickly. The school I attended during my freshman and sophomore years was one of the first schools to re-open in New Orleans. Classmates and friends were enrolling in McDonough 35 and having the time of their lives. Not being a part of that action and environment cut deeply and forced me to miss out on irreplaceable memories.

Moving away from home during the aftermath of Hurricane Katrina made me realize how much I would be sacrificing to chase my dreams. I sacrificed immediate gratification for my long-term goals. Slidell was back up and running before New Orleans and had a few fast-food places open. The re-opened businesses were paying higher than usual because of supply and demand and a shortage of workers.

The minimum wage in 2006 was $5.15 an hour, but I made $12 an hour working at KFC after the storm. Relatively speaking, that wage was great at the time because most of my peers were jobless or earned near minimum wage. On top of that, my co-workers and I were having the time of our lives working at the fast-food restaurant. However, the fun and newfound income weren't worth sacrificing the new opportunity.

While I was in Slidell, my mother was in Atlanta, Georgia. She mentioned the idea of moving to Houston. Reconnecting with my mom helped me get recentered and gave me a slight sense of normalcy during uncertain times.

It took us several months to find housing. Living in a Hilton hotel on Southwest Freeway in Houston was one of the most chaotic scenarios I experienced. The lobby of the Hilton remained full as if we were in a public housing development. Rules were a thing of the past.

Patrons and employees were breaking numerous rules in broad daylight, but the employees were needed because of the excess evacuees. Hanging out by the bar was one of my favorite places to chill at the hotel. A group of rowdy guys from New Orleans served as my entertainment. They hung around the bar and gambled in the hallway nearby.

The bartender was into gambling also. A guy named Jermaine from New Orleans with long dreadlocks and gold teeth used to give the bartender a hard time every time they crossed paths. The bartender was built like a recycling bin, and Jermaine always joked about how the bartender was shaped. Jermaine lacked height but not a voice. Loudcapping was his way of talking and trying to embarrass someone. Everyone could tell that the bartender was tired of his games.

A common mindset most guys from New Orleans share is that we think no one is tougher than us. That was the mentality needed to protect ourselves, where fighting and low-blow verbal insults are common practices amongst close friends. However, many people didn't take well to that in Houston.

When Jermaine found out that the bartender liked to gamble, he joked about how he would take the bartender's money. Apparently, that struck a nerve because the bartender asked someone to cover for him while he accepted the challenge to a dice game. The bartender quickly followed the group from New Orleans to the gambling area, and I trailed behind them. When a circle formed, the bartender dropped a $20 bill on the floor and said, "Shoot for $20."

Ones and fives were on the floor, but the loudmouth didn't back down. He pulled out five twenties, and the bartender collected $80 in four rolls. When the loudmouth got down to his last $20, he did several things to get the bartender out of his rhythm. Jermaine tricked the bartender out of his point three times and wound up winning $200 from him.

I thought things were over until Jermaine threw money in the bartender's direction as if he was a stripper and said, "Go make me a fucking drink!"

The bartender stepped on the money and responded, "Ima make you a drink after I whip your ass."

Everyone, including me, followed them outside to watch them fight. The same mouth that was talking shit was filled with blood shortly after they began scrapping in the parking lot. While nursing himself in pain and shame, Jermaine shouted, "You're a dead man walking! You're a dead man walking!" as the bartender walked inside to continue his shift. I was worried that there would be retaliation over the next several weeks and could not wait until our stint in the overcrowded and chaotic hotel was over.

Things felt surreal once we moved into an apartment on the southwest side of Houston. The transition to Texas cut deeper when New Orleans was back up and running. Being away from home was a major sacrifice, so I had to make the mission worth it.

I was intentional about my mission as soon as I moved to Houston with India and my mom. My mom knew boxing was my priority, so we drove around the entire city for hours trying to locate a gym that would be the best fit for me. Driving around one of the country's largest and most populated cities was an all-day task, but that didn't deter us. Several days after I began classes at Westside High School, a classmate referred me to Savannah Boxing Gym.

Exposure is the key to new levels. Walking into Savannah Gym was a turning point in my life. Willie Savannah began training fighters in the 1970s and became known for teaching his boxers lessons about boxing and life. He and his wife Clara opened a boxing gym in Southwest Houston. Savannah Gym became a staple for Texas's amateur and professional boxing scene.

People ranging from little kids to professionals were passionately putting in work across the two-story gym. I saw firsthand how champions trained and carried themselves outside the public spotlight. While I watched everyone better themselves at Savannah Boxing Gym, I thought about the fighters back home who had never been exposed to an environment like this.

Your roots can tangle you up if they aren't
trimmed from time to time.

———————

LESSON

CHAPTER 10

The Right Environment

My early days at Savannah Boxing Gym showed me the importance of structure, resources, and environments. Savannah possessed all the resources to provide value to champions, plus the structure to produce more champions. We didn't have a similar boxing environment in New Orleans. Consequently, no boxer from my city had won a world title since 1963, when Willy Pastrano won the WBA Light Heavyweight title.

Becoming a world champion was far off my radar at that time. My mindset in 2007 was to become one of the best amateur boxers in Houston and see where the grind would take me. Regardless of my natural gifts and fearless tenacity, I was far behind my peers when I started boxing at Savannah.

Most of the fighters I was grouped with had been fighting for several years or more. They received professional training while I sharpened my skills fighting on the streets. An untrained eye could tell that I was fighting differently from the other amateur boxers. Nonetheless, Coach Savannah took me in as a fighter in his gym and didn't charge me to train there when I first started.

It's said that if a person can make it out of New Orleans, they can make it anywhere on Earth. Although my peers had more technical skills, I knew I could hurt them more than they could hurt me. Learning that there was more to boxing than hurting my opponent became one of my toughest growing pains during my amateur career.

I felt good about finishing third in a state tournament until I couldn't bite a peanut M&M on the ride back to Houston. Being impervious to pain led me to taking punches when I didn't have to. Defense had to be a focal point going forward.

Being in the right environment gave me the right opportunity to develop. I had several sparring partners on higher levels. Aside from an official boxing match, there is no better way to develop than sparring. An athlete can do drills until they're blue in the face, but nothing replicates live action.

I didn't have that opportunity in my previous boxing environment. Besides Red, I'd be lucky to find a decent sparring partner every now and then. Most of the time, they were in different weight classes or skill levels. Being from a different environment benefited me in unexpected ways.

I didn't fit in with any group when I first started at the gym. Most of the fighters had been cliqued up for several years, and I was the new face in the facility. Rocking alone and being cordial with others helped me become a sponge and gave me the freedom to socialize and learn from everyone in the gym.

The different groups rarely paid attention to people outside of their cliques, but I had the opportunity to pay attention to everyone. Having friends is important, but utilizing discernment before letting someone into your life or circle is even more important.

There were plenty of people from New Orleans who attended Westside High also. High school is the proverbial fork in the road for most people. I had already chosen my route before graduation and began adapting to the boxing lifestyle. On school days, I worked out and jogged before sunrise. During classes, my mind was on boxing. At night, I would be at Savannah or grinding at home.

Reflecting on my change of environment helped me see the beauty in one of the ugliest storms in world history. My life finally became structured after it fell apart. Changing environments transitioned me from being a big fish in a little pond to a little fish in an ocean. Red was the only person I was trying to catch up to in New Orleans. However, there were plenty of fighters in my gym, city, and state ahead of me in Texas.

The boxing scene in Houston reminded me of the football scene in New Orleans. Louisiana is always at the top of the list of producing professional football players. There is no shortage of resources for football players of all levels, but boxing resources are scarce in my hometown.

Knowing someone who made it from your environment provides a unique spark of motivation. It's one thing to see a person prosper, but it's another thing to see a prosperous person who walked in your shoes. I was always inspired by people who made it big from New Orleans, but none of them were boxers.

Who knows how much faster I would have transcended and gotten into boxing if Muhammad Ali, Mike Tyson, or Sugar Ray Leonard were from New Orleans? It was Detroit native Joe Louis who inspired a pipeline of fighters from Michigan like Tommy Hearns, Floyd Mayweather Jr. & Sr., James Toney, Clarissa Shields, Alycia Baumgardner, and plenty of others. Other historic fighters have done the same for their respective states. I envisioned myself becoming a boxing pioneer for New Orleans.

Knowing fighters my age with more than ten years of experience under their belt made me realize how far behind I was. Starting boxing late stacked the odds of succeeding against me. Most of my peers were on the verge of turning pro and signing lucrative promotional deals when I was just beginning. It was exciting to be around their buzz, but I didn't confuse my timing with theirs.

While learning the fundamentals and becoming a student of the game, I began devising a plan to overcome my disadvantages. My parents cultivated a culture of hard work in the household. Working double shifts was a way of life for my mother. My dad preached that my work ethic would be the way I could surpass other boxers. Having something to focus on after Katrina expedited my recovery process. The pain from knowing my life would never be the same again was heavy on my heart, but having boxing on my mind helped me channel it.

I had two starts in boxing, one in Houston and one in New Orleans. I didn't have a vivid vision for myself at the beginning. When I started in Houston, I wanted to become one of the best in Texas, but not many others saw that happening. Being an outcast in a new environment helped me gravitate closer to my first manager and consistent trainer, Tee. He saw my potential, was from New Orleans, and could relate to me better than the other trainers who were around.

I began making the most of my environment by studying my surroundings. There were several people I looked up to at my gym. A friend who trained at Savannah was one of the most gifted fighters I ever witnessed. He had such a feel for the sport that he could hold conversations while sparring and give me valuable lessons about being a southpaw.

Your roots can tangle you up if they aren't trimmed from time to time. My friend's boxing ability wasn't the only reason I looked up to him. He and I had something other than boxing in common. My friend was a hometown hero who relocated to Houston to take his career to new levels.

Shortly after relocating, he won a medal at the Olympics. That historic accomplishment propelled his career to new heights. After becoming an Olympian and signing a contract worth more than $1 million, my friend appeared to have a clear path to stardom.

He was compensated six figures for several of his first few pro fights. My friend came from poverty, like most other fighters. Even if he came from a silver spoon, earning over one million dollars for your signature is a remarkable experience, especially as a teenager.

That signature also came with a lot of responsibilities and expectations. When we sign up for obligations, it's imperative for us to know what comes with that commitment. That price tag came with an enormous amount of pressure from all angles. Analysts compared him to the greats before a meaningful belt was wrapped around his waist. Regardless of the pressure, he was delivering in the ring. The only person that could stop him was himself. He did just that when he caught several felony charges for allegedly trafficking narcotics.

On the outside looking in, it's easy to judge him on his mishap. Many outsiders can't grasp the pressure that stars from impoverished backgrounds face. Pressure from family and friends is a part of the deal, but there are deeper forms of pressure.

A lucrative sports contract comes with the expectation that an athlete will instantly leave their past life behind and walk a straight line to stay out of trouble. Young athletes are asked to grow up and mature with the stroke of a pen. Time and obstacles are two of the most important elements of growth, and prodigies aren't awarded much of either.

Family, friends, and people he barely knew pulled him away from boxing to aid their personal pleasures. I highly doubt that it was my friend's idea to flip his boxing money in the drug game. People with money are constantly approached by people with passionate ideas and no money. Not being able to say no has cost plenty of people their fortune.

If they gave him support and time to develop, he would have been able to provide more for them. He was always looking out for others financially once he started getting paid, although only a few people looked out for him when he was broke. His detrimental surroundings made me conceptualize how important a support system is. If others around him supported his dream, it wouldn't have been short-lived.

Boxing isn't a career where a criminal record can hold you back. I am not sure how my friend's grind was after he got incarcerated, but it's hard to imagine him growing at the same pace outside of Savannah. When he returned to the gym, he still had skills, but it was an uphill battle trying to recapture his magic. Straddling the streets and boxing was an everlasting battle with him. The pop in his punches wasn't the same, nor was his level of motivation.

Boxing isn't a sport you can play. You must live boxing. Being ten-toes down is the way of life for successful boxers. One or two toes off the ledge can be the reason for someone's downfall.

My friend's shortcomings showed me that discipline will take you places motivation can't. He had the motivation and talent to accomplish everything he wanted to in the sport, but his lack of discipline destroyed his dreams. Most habits from your old environment won't translate to the new environment you desire.

My persistence as a child seamlessly translated into adulthood. I stopped at no cost to get what I wanted and always saw obstacles as barriers I could overcome. Persistence and stubbornness go hand-in-hand, and both are needed if you want to successfully go against the grain. My parents molded me to become a scholar and college student. I always had a passion for learning, but I wasn't interested in furthering my formal education after high school.

The balance of my mother's tough love and my father's nurturing cultivated my balance of empathy and aggression. My aggression outweighed empathy when determining my path after high school. Many teenagers follow the path their parents want them to take because they empathize with the sacrifices their parents made to help them get to that point.

I appreciated my parents' sacrifices, but I didn't want to take a regrettable road and follow someone else's dream. There is nothing wrong with college, but I knew it wasn't for me. Knowing something isn't for you and still going through with it is a regret waiting to happen.

Moving to Houston was the entryway of my tunnel vision for boxing, but my parents insisted I explore another avenue. While peers younger than me at the gym were turning pro, my parents wanted me to enroll in college. I honored their wishes and enrolled at Texas Southern University after finishing high school in May 2007.

Proof that moving to Houston would be best for me happened the summer after my high school graduation. After Hurricane Katrina, Primo and I hung out with a crew that consisted of Slim, Greg, and Lenny. Primo and I were the wildest ones, and Slim was the least likely to get in trouble. His father was active in his life and strict about everything his son did. Slim's involvement wouldn't go much further than a lookout. The incident that changed his life forever showed me how detrimental being at the wrong place at the wrong time and hanging with the wrong people can be.

Back in Slidell, the group Primo and I used to hang with continued hanging together without us after we moved away. I felt left out occasionally, but this incident reminded me that I was in the right place. We would get into fights with others and go out all night long when I lived there, but things changed after my departure.

A new person in the group allegedly brought them on a robbery without them knowing. Slim would be scared to take something if no one was looking. I know he got the short end of the stick of a wrong place - wrong time scenario and didn't intend to harm anyone. The court and jury didn't consider that during his trial. The botched robbery led to a fatality, and everyone in the group received a lengthy prison sentence. One of the defendants committed suicide, and Slim is still incarcerated, trying to prove his innocence. I was convinced that Texas was the right environment for me.

When we are evolving, it's best to hang
with people who've already evolved.

_____

LESSON

CHAPTER 11

Close Calls

I received a wake-up call, but wasn't fully woke yet. When we are evolving, it's best to hang with people who've already evolved. Before training at Savannah, I didn't have many friends who were boxers.

Connecting with Jermell and Jermall Charlo changed that. Our bond is deeper than boxing. We went to parties together, caught the bus together, and spent the night at each other's houses. Shedding blood, sweat, and tears together at the boxing gym wasn't the only aspect of our brotherhood.

Their father's support reminded me of my dad's support. He boxed and had his boys focused and on point at a young age about how to function in and out of the ring. One day, Jermell helped me realize that I had more growing to do outside the ring.

While in traffic together, someone almost hit us with their car. I was already enraged about how the driver almost carelessly caused a wreck, but things went further after we got into a verbal altercation. He began mouthing off about how he would bat me in my mouth. Their car was filled with people, but the driver and I agreed to meet down the street to fight.

Once I pulled off to pick up some more friends to fight, Jermell tapped me on the knee and said, "Bring me home dog."

His smart decision didn't stop me from getting into a brawl that day, but it inspired me to grow out of my old ways of fighting on the streets. That situation could have easily turned out worse.

Jermell was also there for one of my most embarrassing moments. Have you ever dated someone you knew you shouldn't have been dating? That's how I felt about Crystal.

She had already been put out by her mother at 16 and developed a shiesty reputation. Her big sister took her in. The two sisters dated a pair of brothers when they lived in New Orleans before the hurricane. Apparently, that relationship wasn't left in the past like she claimed.

One evening after training, I asked Jermell to drop me off at Crystal's place. She and I occasionally got into it, but we reached a new level of turmoil when I entered her place and saw another man in her bed. The guy she claimed to be done with was napping in her bed on a Friday evening. His brother was napping nearby, but I still went left field on them.

I forgot Jermell was still outside until the two guys left, and I went back outside. He asked me if I wanted to leave several times, but I had already been sweet-talked against my better judgment and decided to stay.

Even though I fell victim to her games that night, I dodged a bullet by not being with her for the long run. After we broke up, her sister's boyfriend went to jail for a few years. When he was locked up, Crystal kept in touch and always referred to him as her brother. Down the line, Crystal got pregnant, and no one knew who the father was until her son was in pre-school. Her child has the same face as her sister's ex-boyfriend.

...

By 2008, I made progress as an amateur boxer, but I still felt far away from my goals and wasn't far removed from street activity. My love for my sister is deeper than words could explain. Aside from being her protector and best friend, I always felt responsible for leading her in the right direction. I knew India wasn't too far behind each step I took. We were in a new city and environment, so she watched my moves even closer.

On Fridays, some friends and I would steal from a store in West Oaks Mall. Almost everything is 30 minutes apart in Houston, and I was usually responsible for giving my sister a ride whenever she needed one. When I wasn't available a few Fridays in a row, I told her what I had been up to. My sister was surprised at first, but life was so chaotic after the storm that she didn't judge me.

I would bring several friends to the mall and steal from a store that sold all their merchandise for $7.95. They would give you an oversized bag even if you purchased one item. One of us would go into the store to purchase an item. Then we would re-enter the store, stuff that bag, and get away every time.

Boxing pulled me away from the foolishness. Others knew about the operation and went on missions without me. Guilt hit me in the face when India called to tell me that she and a friend named Brittney got caught stealing in the same store I used to steal from.

I dropped what I was doing and sped to the mall. When I entered the "holding cell" at the mall, my sister and her friend were sitting with their hands cuffed behind chairs. I pleaded for the security officer to let them go, and he eventually obliged. Once the security guard leaned down to remove the handcuffs from Brittney's wrist, she farted in his face.

I did everything I could to hold my laugh in, but I began crying laughing once India and Brittney started laughing. Everyone found it funny except the mall cop, who instantly had a sore throat after that experience.

Once he finished choking, he raised his raspy voice and said, "I was going to let you two go without getting in trouble, but since you all find shit funny, one of your parents will have to come to get you!"

My sister's run-in ended up being a laughable experience, but I was rattled internally. She made a wrong move because I behaved outside of my character. Aside from my routine scuffles, I hadn't gotten in any real trouble, and neither had she.

When my funds were insufficient, I stepped even further out of my lane. Poor circumstances often influence poor choices. Ends became even harder to meet as my amateur career advanced. I picked up a side hustle that could have landed me in prison or ended my life.

I gave my roommate a heads-up that I might be short on next month's rent, and he told me about an opportunity to make money. He had a connect on pills for a cheap price and convinced me that it would be a smart idea to make some quick money to cover our bills. His way of hustling was by scamming people and fraud, so I would be getting into this game with no guidance or wingman.

I got the pills for $8 a piece and sold them for $20. More than doubling my investment and not having to bust my ass for money was convenient for me. I had beginner's luck and made several flips, but eventually, I became the worst drug dealer ever.

One of my closest calls occurred while I was furthest away from my calling. There was minimal time for boxing when I started working at FedEx. To accommodate my training schedule and classes at Texas Southern University, I began working 3:00 AM shifts. The graveyard hours gig wasn't my primary source of income, selling pills was.

All steps forward aren't in the right direction. I thought I was getting ahead by making fast money, but that was a misconception. I was one move away from taking a step forward and several steps back. That move happened one Friday summer afternoon.

Robberies were common in my neighborhood. On this evening, law enforcement was on the prowl for three suspects who committed a string of armed robberies in the area earlier that day. I just so happened to be riding in that same area with my friends Jordan and Marco.

The police tracked us down like we were on the most wanted list. They rode my bumper for several blocks around the corner from my house. While we debated what we should do over a Lil Wayne mixtape, the police cut their lights on.

The flashing red and blue lights and sirens caused my heart to drop. I had a lengthy prison sentence worth of pills in the backseat, and everyone in the car knew it. The police cornered us in too quickly for me to do anything about the narcotics. It would be up to God and my friend in the back seat to save us.

I was already accustomed to getting stopped by the police. However, nothing could prepare me for what came next. After we were pulled over, two police officers hurried to my front doors with their guns drawn and yelled, "Get out with your hands up!"

Marco and I were forcefully led to the back seat of a police car. Jordan was in cuffs also, but he hadn't been placed in a police car yet. I didn't know if he was acting as our lawyer or an informant while the police pressed him.

After they started talking, several police cars hurried onto the scene, and two helicopters hovered over us. I began visualizing everything I worked and sacrificed for going down the drain once K9s emerged from one of the squad cars to inspect our vehicle.

I thought it was over for us until someone on the officer's radio said, "That's not them! They were in a green car, and two of them had face tattoos. We just spotted them on Bissonnet!"

The dogs appeared more disappointed than the police. The cops knew we weren't robbers, but the dogs knew something they couldn't articulate. Jordan cut a hole in my backseat to hide my pills and didn't tell on me when the police pressed him. This chapter of my life would have taken a turn for the worse if he didn't have my back under pressure.

My stubbornness translated to the streets. Shortly after my close call with the police, I encountered a situation that could have ended it all. One customer represented 50% of my clientele. I would get the pills in Houston and drive them to New Orleans. He was deep into the streets and bought half my stash every time I came to town.

Usually, he texted me on Thursday to put in his order before I got on the road to leave. Instead of texting this Thursday, he called. Before I could say hello, he said, "Yeah, Regis. Hold on right quick. My lil potna wants to holla at you bout those pills, ya heard me?"

Once I responded, "Okay," the darkest voice I ever heard said, "Yeah, I need to link with you. When you get in town, pull up on me with all your pills."

I thought an explanation or introduction would come before or after that, but he hung up. A few of my friends pleaded for me not to meet up with him. The guy I was going to meet sold every drug in the book and beat robbery and murder charges. It felt like I was driving toward the end of a cliff and couldn't make a turn.

The guy I was supposed to meet up with changed the location several times before we were supposed to link. He led me to a deserted road with broken streetlights. As soon as I parked, he quickly glided toward my passenger door. He was wearing a black hoody during the summertime and kept his hands in his hoody pocket until he extended his right hand and said, "Wazzam?"

When our hands shook, mine caught a chill. He picked up from where he left off on the phone and said, "Like I was saying, I need all of the pills you have. Ima look out for you after I flip that."

His hands remained in his pockets, and I didn't see any cash, so I asked, "Where is the money?"

He leaned toward me and said, "It's going to be in your hands after you put me on with the pills."

I don't know if it just sounded persuasive at the moment or if I knew he was considering brandishing the gun, I saw poking out of his pocket. When he exited the car with my pills, I knew I was jacked, but I was thankful to make it through that life-threatening situation.

When I was young, my dad told me I had a spirit guiding my life. I didn't conceptualize it until situations that could have damaged my future reversed course at the last minute. I knew my Uncle Regis played a factor in guiding my good fortune.

On the following Monday morning, I gained a new angel. While getting dressed at the boxing gym, my mind was on how my encounter in the streets could have taken a turn for the worse. My mind should have been on boxing, but that's an example of how your real-life actions can creep into your craft. Some people don't learn until it's too late, and their vices or bad habits take them down.

Typically, I leave my phone in the car when I go to the gym, but this morning, I brought it in with me. While putting it in my bag before practice, a friend called. I planned on calling her back after I left the gym until she reached out three times.

When I answered, a friend grievingly yelled, "Cedric was killed this morning!"

The pain in her voice and her tears confirmed the tragedy. Cedric held a special place in people's hearts, including mine. I silently took a seat on the floor while my friend continued through her sobs and asked, "You there? You there?"

I don't recall my rebuttal, but I remembered how it felt when my heart shattered after getting the news. Many memories crossed my mind while the pain expounded through my body, and I fought to suppress the tears. The first flashback was him nodding at me in the locker room, letting me know that boxing was for me.

Getting the news on a Monday morning tested my mental strength and emotional endurance. After hearing about my friend's tragic and violent death, I knew the pain would linger. It was hard to carry on with the rest of my day. Grown men were about to be swinging full speed and strength at my head in the following minutes, and I couldn't afford for my mind to be in too many other places.

Losing friends to gun violence at a young age became a normalcy. During that era, numbness began developing due to repeated tragedies. Donald, my first amateur opponent, and several other friends I grew up with died from gun violence around the same time Cedric was killed.

Losing Cedric and Donald made me realize how much boxing played a factor in my life. Fighting connected us on different levels. I know Cedric would have been one of my biggest supporters if he was still alive. The confidence he bestowed in me lived on even stronger after his death.

REGIS PROGRAIS

Regis is gone — world loses a blithe spirit

Regis Prograis had a line he used for those well-meaning, ridiculous people who hang around hospitals and ask sick little boys what they will be when they grow up.

"I don't know, lady," he would say, pointing at the row of plasma bottles attached to his arms. "But I think I could turn out to be a vampire here."

Regis Prograis won't be turning out to be a vampire. And Regis won't be getting any more of the shocked, embarrassed laughter he loved to get with that line. Detroit's strongest, smartest and least cynical practitioner of grim humor died of leukemia at his northwest Detroit home Wednesday night. He was 12.

"He knew it was time, and he just seemed to fade away," his mother, Mrs. Theresa Prograis, said yesterday. "He didn't want any bother, no trouble for anybody. It was just like the way he lived."

A person can only get so far if their corner
doesn't believe in them.

_____

LESSON

CHAPTER 12

Confidence

Have you ever seen a salesperson miss a sale and confidently keep going until they secure the next sale, or a basketball player miss several shots in a row but keep shooting with confidence? Persistence positions them to become confident winners. They are different from salespeople who are afraid to pitch their product, and basketball players who are scared to take their next shot.

Confidence isn't something we are born with. It's something developed over time by repeated actions. My belief in myself was always unshakable, but my confidence was tested early in my career.

One of the first big-name opponents I faced outside of Savannah Gym is considered one of the best boxers of my generation. My confidence wasn't tested by facing him. The test came from my corner.

Moments before the fight, my trainer gave me a game plan on what to do if it felt like I was about to get knocked out. My opponent knocked out each competitor he faced in the tournament, and we were matched up for the finals.

My confidence remained intact for our close fight, but I wasn't sure about my corner anymore. I made an impressive showing, but my trainer didn't. A person can only get so far if their corner doesn't believe in them.

Confidence is the most important characteristic for a boxer to possess. You'll be hard-pressed to find a boxer who doesn't think they can knock anyone out or beat them. I felt a type of way about someone in my corner doubting me, but I quickly gained reassurance from another source.

Tee's confidence in me balanced things out, but led me to my first mistake in the business aspect of boxing. He invited me and another friend I trained with to his house. Tee gave us a pitch that we were closer to making money in boxing, and he had an opportunity to help us advance our careers. He presented us with contracts. We trusted Tee and didn't have any reservations about stopping ourselves from signing something he said was beneficial for us.

As an amateur, I signed a deal to be managed by Tee once I turned pro. That was illegal, and I was committed to him for a certain amount of time and fights. Shortly after I signed the deal, I realized it was a bad one.

Going to court is one of the quickest ways to stall a boxer's career. The plaintiff won't be able to fight during the case. The defendant or court could prolong the case and contribute to one of a boxer's biggest detriments - layoff time.

The unstable ground I was living on shifted further when more boxers at Savannah began turning pro. Business conflicts altered the morale of the gym. I was disappointed when everyone went their separate ways, but I was thankful for my experience at the legendary gym.

Signing a contract at the time seemed like a symbol of career advancement, but it was the opposite. An opportunity for real career advancement came during the Golden Gloves tournament. Winning the tournament positions amateurs for endorsements and is a resume-building accomplishment. Unfortunately, I lost in the finals to David Williams, a name I will never forget.

Pro fights and amateur fights are scored differently. In the amateurs, you can beat up your opponent, but still lose if they land more punches. I landed the harder shots, but David Williams landed more.

I was transparent with myself about where I was in my career and vowed to see him again on a bigger stage with a different outcome. He became a target and measuring stick for my growth.

I simultaneously found out that college and working a job weren't for me. Most of my days started with work before daybreak and ended after midnight once I trained beyond exhaustion. Having a roommate with a different lifestyle furthered my desire for a change.

After my roommate and I could no longer keep up with the bills, we went our separate ways, and I moved in with my mother. My mom and I grew closer each day, and I enjoyed the experience of living with her. I never imagined us being in that situation, but I appreciated it.

Pressure began creeping in because I dropped out of college, and was living under my mother's roof. My mom had already sacrificed to buy me a car and take me in, but I knew her support could only get me so far as a man.

I was confident that boxing would pay off down the road, but I needed some form of income to bridge the gap in the meantime. Doing anything illegal was out of the question. I learned quickly from my mistakes and rarely made them twice.

My faith in the future helped me see
past my current circumstances.

———————

LESSON

CHAPTER 13

Bridging The Gap

I worked several dead-end hustles, and it felt like I was hustling backward. I never lost hope, but this day was the closest I ever came to losing it. After delivering newspapers in 100-degree weather, I prayed to God for a sign.

While my head rested on the hot steering wheel, an enthusiastic voice blasted through the speakers and asked, "Do you like fitness? Do you like being in the gym? Do you want to help others reach their fitness goals? Well, sign up to take our course and become a personal trainer!"

Have you ever been to church, and it felt like the sermon was intended for you or thought about someone, and then they called you? That's what it felt like when God sent me a message on a historically hot summer day in 2008. The advertisement informed me about an opportunity I hadn't considered. I hurried home to submit my paperwork to enroll in courses to become a personal trainer. Getting paid for something I loved doing alleviated some stress and lifted a heavy burden off my shoulders.

Stress shifted from my shoulders onto my mother's shoulders. India moved back to New Orleans after she finished high school. My mom always invited India to come live with her after she left. India took her up on that offer when she became pregnant with my first nephew, Kayden. India, Kayden, and his father moved in with my mother and me.

It's ironic how I experienced some of my most joyous moments during some of my toughest times. My faith in the future helped me see past my current circumstances. I was sleeping on the floor next to my mother's bed, barely had two nickels to rub together, and my future was uncertain. While there were many things to be sad about in my new environment, I established a friendship that developed into a brotherhood and experienced priceless memories with my family that I wouldn't trade for the world.

Until I met Benji, most of my friends were around my age or older. I met him when he was ten years old, and I was 19. We were at different stages in our lives, but still established a strong and priceless bond from day one. He is the third youngest of seven, and his family was from the Lafite projects in New Orleans. Most of them lived in the apartment complex with us.

My new community reminded me of my neighborhood in New Orleans East. Everyone was outside, ranging from little kids to senior citizens. Most people my age was already in the streets and began traveling down the wrong path.

Regardless of my daring ways, I knew my limits in the streets. I never wanted to be a man of the streets or a gangster because the ones I grew up around were on the block all day, didn't have sustainable lifestyles, and experienced unhealable trauma. Their reputations were solid in the neighborhood, but that could only get them so far, and I wanted to go further than that. Having that mutual desire and vision with Benji helped us develop a bond even though we were at two different stages in our lives. Our mindset helped us bridge the gap between our ages.

It was a blessing to have most of my family under one roof, but even the happiest family would bump heads if five of them lived in a 500-square-foot one-bedroom apartment in the hood. Minor conflicts were inevitable. My mom worked two jobs at the time as she did most of her career. That was already a mentally and physically taxing grind. My mother could be bill-less and living a life of luxury, but would still feel the need to pull a double shift. That's fitting for my current grind, so reflecting gives me a deeper appreciation for the work ethic she helped instill in me.

Our work ethics kept us out of the house most of the time, but our time there wasn't optimal for a home's true use. Your home should be your haven and source of peace and rejuvenation. Sleeping on the floor after grueling boxing workouts and ten-hour workdays didn't create any room for rejuvenation. My mom had her own challenges with the household and decided to throw in the towel.

One evening, she came home and calmly delivered the news that she was moving out. My mom set a date, but we didn't take her seriously until that day came, and she exited the apartment with her belongings to move back to New Orleans.

Some relationships must be sacrificed to achieve our goals. Those relationships don't include our soulmates, children, loved ones, and closest friends, although they must have some understanding of our sacrifices.

———

LESSON

CHAPTER 14

Sink or Swim

My mom has done a countless number of meaningful and magnificent things for me. Aside from birthing me, leaving me in a sink or swim situation was the best thing she ever did for me.

Now, I was spontaneously accountable for grown-man responsibilities. My big brother tendencies always made me feel accountable for my sister. Being there for her in a time of need gave my life a higher level of seriousness and accountability. It took a mature mindset to learn my next lesson in boxing.

My communication with God has always been the most intimate aspect of my life. I always asked Him to help me navigate my life, but not my boxing career. Things changed with how I communicated with Him during an amateur tournament.

An event hosted by the San Antonio Police Department provided amateur boxers with the rare opportunity to receive compensation. Typically, amateurs must pay to participate in tournaments. The contestants who finished at the top would earn prize money and monthly residuals. Those financial rewards meant a lot to me at the time.

Training hard was always a minimum for me, but we all know when we could have gone an extra rep or minute while working out. Other times, we could simply be undeserving of an opportunity. Delusion and inability to self-assess block many people from being able to see this point of view. I was already playing catch-up in boxing, so I needed to be firing on all cylinders during my preparation and execution for amateur fights.

I felt like the student who prayed for an A on an exam they weren't fully prepared for after the fight ended. I busted my ass to prepare, but wasn't sure if I deserved the victory. Right before the winner of the fight and money was revealed, I clenched my eyes and prayed to God that I would come out victorious.

God taught me several lessons when the referee dropped my hand and raised my opponent's hand. I felt selfish praying for the outcome of a fight while other people were starving, homeless, fighting diseases, and living through war. God doesn't have a favorite boxer or sports team. Saying more prayers than my opponent wouldn't have propelled me to victory. We have to meet God halfway with some of the things we pray for, especially prayers and goals that require effort and dedication. Why should God select you for an opportunity instead of someone else who wants the same thing and worked harder to get it?

That didn't stop my boxing-related prayers. It just shifted them. I began praying for the health and safety of my opponent and me in the ring. Those prayers have kept my opponents and me safe, and I will continue saying them. I never prayed for a victory again after that amateur fight.

The next lesson I learned as an amateur was less complex but equally as important. Following instructions is an underrated way to stay out of trouble. I had been looking forward to the 2009 Golden Gloves tournament more than any amateur tournament. This was primed to be my breakout. I was a favorite to win the prestigious event. After weigh-ins, my manager was adamant about me not leaving. Moments after he told me not to leave, I left.

I was starving and thought I could return before he noticed. My friend and I didn't make it two blocks before we were pulled over. I regretted letting him drive my car while the police approached us. He chose that time to tell me about his warrants.

My friend's warrants were in Louisiana, and mine were in the same county we were pulled over in. The officer didn't want to hear that I had a boxing tournament about to start or that I would pay my tickets on Monday. I had several unpaid traffic tickets, and the mindset of "catch me if you can" when it came to paying them. Unfortunately, they caught me at the worst time.

I was pulled over and arrested in front of a LA Fitness while a significant break in my career was supposed to be taking place. I shook my head in disbelief almost the entire ride to the police station. I had even more reasons to shake my head when I made it to the holding cell.

We were packed in there like sardines in a can, and the cell was cold enough to preserve meat. My boxing outfit caused all types of unwanted conversations. Multiple people began trying to impress me. One inmate told me he sparred with Muhammad Ali, but didn't know the difference between a southpaw and an orthodox. Another inmate claimed to be a kingpin, but couldn't afford to pay $100 for his freedom.

As the clock ticked, my anger boiled. I had false hope that I would be released early enough to return for my first fight. I knocked myself out of the tournament and was still behind bars when it ended.

On top of squandering the career-changing opportunity, I hadn't eaten in almost two days. During the entire evening and night in jail, I told myself I wouldn't fall asleep there. When the clock struck 3:00 AM, I laid my head on my shoes and fell asleep.

...

My mother's departure sped up my maturation process for the most part. However, that level of seriousness hadn't translated to all areas of my life. I had a girlfriend at the time,

114

but I wasn't ten toes down in our relationship. The proof came when I reconnected with a girl named Tatianna, I knew from the boxing gym.

My girlfriend at the time was an amazing person and checked off all the boxes for wife material. Despite her being a catch, the situation didn't hold my undivided attention. Our different backgrounds were the only missing element in our relationship.

I traded eight things I liked about one woman for two things I liked about another. Tatianna looked amazing and cooked like a master chef. Our list of commonalities stopped there, but I still made time for her.

I made time for Tatianna during one of the worst times possible. I invited her over one night shortly after India and I moved into a new place. My girlfriend didn't live there, but she had a key and stopped by periodically.

Several knocks at the door woke Tatianna and I up the following morning. When I peeked through the blinds, I loudly whispered for India to hook the chain lock. Once my sister made it to the door, my girlfriend had already inserted her spare key. Before she could turn the doorknob, India secured the chain lock.

While my girlfriend dialed my number on the doorstep and my side chick laid in my bed, I escaped through the back door. After sprinting around the block, I greeted my girlfriend on the steps. I felt guilty about my situation inside, but even more guilty about holding a woman's life up because I couldn't be what she needed me to be. We had no choice but to part ways.

My relationship with Tatianna caused collateral damage. Initially, I promised my sister the bigger room in our new two-bedroom apartment, but I backtracked on my word once I started being a simp for my new boo. I moved Tatianna and her child in shortly after we started talking. Tatianna tried establishing some peace in the household by furnishing most of the apartment, but the peace didn't last long.

We consistently argued about things we would forget about by the end of the day. I didn't know what stress was until I met her. An unforgettable altercation would be our last.

At the time, I misunderstood support in a relationship. I thought providing her a place to stay and not pulling each other away from our lifestyles was a supportive relationship. Tatianna was a woman of the streets, but I didn't try to stop her from going out.

Tatianna planned on going out one Saturday night while I remained inside. Typically, I watched Redbox movies or whatever fight was on television, but my father gave me something new to watch. My dad sent me a DVD of the fight between Marvin Hagler and Tommy Hearns.

Their fight, better known as "The War," is one of the most historic fights in boxing history. Watching that fight was on my mind throughout the entire week. I wouldn't get time to watch it until Tatianna went out with her friends that Saturday night.

I was more excited for them to go out than they were. Our apartment was where Tatianna pre-gamed with her friends, Gerald and Kia, before going out. While they hung out in the living room, I noticed a little tension between Gerald and Kia. They had been dating for several years, and fussing was a primary part of their relationship. Therefore, I didn't pay it much mind. It was entertainment until I could watch the fight that had been on my mind the entire week.

The fight only lasted three rounds, but it has been utilized by college professors to teach lessons, and books were written about it. Watching them go toe to toe was like a front-row seat for a fireworks show on New Year's Eve. Every time I replayed the fight, I saw something new. While cleaning the DVD so it could play clearer, another set of fireworks was about to explode.

Once Gerald marched through my front door like he paid the bills there, he yelled, "Give me the phone right now, Tatianna!"

Tatianna moved in my direction, then responded, "I can't give you a phone I ain't got."

Kia doubled down on that energy and request. Once Tatianna remained adamant that she didn't have it, everyone stared at me. Tatianna wanted me to defend her, and Kia and

Gerald wanted me to help get the phone back. After an awkward silence persisted, Kia shouted, "Girl! You have ten seconds to give me my phone back!"

Before she could start counting, Gerald said, "It's alright. She could keep that phone. We'll take this television."

Gerald walked toward my television and wrapped his arms around it. He was well aware of my hands, so it didn't take long for him to gather himself and behave accordingly. Although he didn't want any smoke, Kia did. She just had it for the wrong person.

When her countdown got to two, Tatianna shouted, "Why don't I countdown to tell Gerald how you spent the night at Barry's house last Monday night instead of mine? How about I tell him how a sugar daddy bought you that purse you wore tonight instead of your uncle?"

Before Tatianna could finish her rant, Kia swung at her. While Gerald and I separated them, I rhetorically asked myself, "What the fuck am I doing?" I was involved in a scenario that contradicted the lifestyle I wanted. Instead of going to sleep thinking about boxing that night, I was devising an exit strategy from that relationship.

Thankfully, I didn't have to spend much time planning one. A few days later, we began arguing on the phone. Moments after she hung up in my face, she sent me a text informing me that she was moving out.

Throughout the day, I wondered what we would fuss about later. By the time I made it home that evening, it looked like someone robbed the place. For a while, I forgot that Tatianna furnished most of the apartment. When she left, I had no choice but to remember. All I had left was my futon, DVD player, and an outdated television.

Once we went our separate ways, I began noticing a pattern in my life. Most of my obstacles occurred at the perfect timing. I was preparing for the Olympic trials when Tatianna abruptly walked out of my life. Breaking free of a toxic situation gave me a fresh wave of energy.

My father's reemergence in my life happened at the perfect time. I was still in need of guidance. He and I never spoke about his exit. We just picked up from where we left off.

My father was still living in Baton Rouge, but still found ways to make his presence felt when he wasn't there. He sent boxing DVDs and VHS tapes consistently. It felt like Christmas every time I got one in the mail. He further exposed me to boxers I needed to know about, including his favorite fighter, Tommy Hearns. Unsurprisingly, some of our favorite fighters fought during the same era. My dad began showing up to my amateur fights and practices like he did when I was a novice athlete. He was always one of the most valuable members of my corner.

One of the most important lessons I learned from him was secondhand. He typically sent me boxing tapes to watch, but a movie that had nothing to do with boxing altered my point of view on relationships. I spent valuable time with women I didn't see a future with. As a result, I was pulling myself away from my dream, but it didn't register in my mind that way until I watched a movie my dad recommended.

The lead character broke up with his high school sweetheart because he felt she would get in the way of his goal. Some clichés don't penetrate past the surface when the context isn't given behind the saying. When the lead character said he would resent his girlfriend if she held him back from achieving his dream of becoming a great musician, I understood his reason for sacrificing the relationship.

Some relationships must be sacrificed to achieve our goals. Those relinquished relationships do not include our soulmates, children, loved ones, and closest friends, although they must have some understanding of our sacrifices. The lead character's girlfriend meant a lot to him, but he didn't love her as much as his craft and wasn't sure if she was his soulmate.

If sacrifice equaled success, the population of greats would be more abundant. Sacrifice must be paired with persistence. It's counterproductive to make sacrifices, but not remain persistent.

My dad helped construct my tunnel vision and molded my mindset to let nothing get in my way. Aside from being the example instead of just the advice, he recommended a movie that enhanced my persistence and affirmed that my sacrifices were worthwhile. After watching that film, I made it a habit to read or watch what someone recommended to me. Most of the time, it's a valuable learning opportunity.

…

One of my biggest wins as an amateur happened outside of an official match. Diego, one of my first trainers, was a boxer from Mexico who just turned pro and was a few years older than me. He moved to Houston as a child and had been friends with his clique at the gym since childhood.

When new fighters started at Savannah Gym, they were assigned a trainer. As boxers develop, other trainers recruit them to partner up and join their stable. Diego trained me for a short amount of time. His primary focus was boxing and making other people laugh at the gym.

My friends and I joke and fight with each other so much that I can easily decipher if someone is joking with me or antagonizing me. I read undertones and slick-hating fluently. Things were copacetic when I first started training with Diego. When he and I were alone, he would do his job with minimal talking.

Once others came around, the jokes began. Other people's reactions influenced how far he went with it. Things never went too far, but they got too consistent for my liking. I would grow aggravated when his entourage was around. He drove me to the point of knowing what I would do if he played with me again.

When I first started training at the gym, I would go to the lockers to get dressed, stretch, and then work out. While I worked out, was Diego's favorite time to mess with me. Eventually, I switched up my routine one day and beat him to the punch.

When I got to the gym on a Friday evening, I went straight to Diego and started messing with him. He was caught off guard, but throwing myself off my routine wasn't worth it. I don't enjoy being petty, but my upbringing molded me to match anyone's pettiness. Therefore, I wanted to settle our beef. Sort of like I did with Kerry behind the tan and white Jordans.

Most people in the gym went to Vegas that weekend for Evander Holyfield's last title victory. I felt a little uneasy about not having the extra money to attend the event, so I decided to put in some extra work while most of the gym was away.

Diego and his crew decided to put in extra work that weekend also. I watched his group's fighting style and respected it. They prided themselves on walking people down in the ring, letting their hands go, and having big kahunas. He would need all of that plus more when I called his hands out after we finished working out that Friday night.

Diego brought it on himself. When I approached him and his friends while he sat on the edge of a ring, he asked me, "No bloody nose today?"

He knew my nose bled easily and that it wasn't a sign of me getting beat up. Nonetheless, he would do and say anything to get a laugh. I shortened the distance between us, took a few steps closer, and snatched the pair of gloves sitting by him. I saw his Adam's apple rise and drop. Then I placed the gloves in his lap and said, "Put your fuckin gloves on and meet me in the ring."

The loud area turned silent until I repeated myself. One of his friends said, "It doesn't sound like he is playing. Whip his ass, so we can hurry up and get out of here tonight."

The days of him showing me the ropes were long gone. I was a few years removed from him training me, and my anger toward him built up. He felt that anger repeatedly on his body and upside his head while I pulverized him in front of his friends. They had no choice but to ooh and ah as their friend got his ass whipped. Hearing their reactions while fucking him up made me unleash on him until they stopped it.

Diego never messed with me again, and I showed him and others how to treat me. Our ability to overcome conflict by throwing hands reminded me of the comradery and beauty bestowed in boxing. That incident turned a rivalry into a friendship.

...

Mindset shifts create some of the most powerful changes in our lives. As I progressed in the amateurs, I started reading more boxing magazines. I fantasized about seeing myself ranked as #1 in them.

One of my favorite times to read them was between clients' training sessions. When a client didn't show up one morning, an article caught my attention. A swimmer no one expected to succeed became an Olympic champion by substituting his TV time for reading. His unconventional method of using his mind to advance at a physical activity intrigued me. I immediately adopted that practice.

During 2011, my confidence reached new heights, and I felt ready for a new level. I finished at the top of each amateur tournament, but knew I had to take care of a few things before turning pro. I needed to avenge my loss to David Williams. This time, when we met, the stakes were higher. He and I were fighting to see who would advance to the Olympic Trials.

If you aren't getting better, you are getting worse. That goes for boxing and real life. Quickly into the fight, I realized he was a copy-and-paste version of himself from the last time we faced each other. He tried hitting me with the same moves, but I wasn't the same fighter. I made that evident by brutally outclassing him and punching my ticket to the Olympic Trials.

I didn't realize how far I came until I defeated someone who beat me and qualified for the trials. I was a few fights away from potentially becoming an Olympian in the 2012 Olympics. Other boxers dreamed of qualifying for the Olympic trials while I was still dreaming about becoming like Kobe Bryant and Allen Iverson.

Surpassing others who started before me boosted my confidence. I knew it was only the beginning, but it didn't feel like I just got started because of how hard I was grinding. Sometimes, it's best to keep your head down and grind.

This stage of my career showed me how imperative it is to redefine the next level of success as you climb. I didn't expect to make it that far in that short amount of time, so it felt like I won already. Consequently, I lost two fights I should have won at the trials. From the beginning, I vowed to work my hardest and see where it took me, but the Olympic Trials exceeded my vision at that time.

Watching boxers from across the world compete during the 2012 Olympics in London expanded my mindset from local to worldwide and ignited a desire to fight in London one day. I knew boxers across the world were training for the same belts, medals, and accolades I desired, so I began devising a plan to outwork them. I finished my amateur career 87-7 and ranked

#4 in the country. The losses quickly rolled off my shoulders because I knew in my heart that it was time to graduate to a new level and turn pro.

The most underrated aspect of the hard road is
the end reward. It's easy to forget how fruitful
the rewards will be while you are getting it out
of the mud, but a seed only blossoms
after it's covered in dirt.

———————

LESSON

CHAPTER 15

Hard Road

The word selfish gets an unfair rap sometimes. I would never vouch for anyone being selfish in the sense of greed for monetary possessions, but people must have seasons of life when they are selfish with their time. As I ascended through my career, my tunnel vision became more concise.

When I was a teenager, I was the first one of my friends to have a car. I prioritized who I was hanging with and often did time-wasting activities. Before I started training in the Lower 9th Ward, I didn't know what me-time was. Previously, I was always with my family or friends.

Once I started identifying more ways to improve, I began carving out more time for myself. By the time I turned pro, I realized how my priorities shifted. My world began revolving around boxing and reading. Wasting time wasn't an activity anymore because I began making the most out of every moment.

The hard road is an applicable and common journey in all walks of life. Entrepreneurs take the hard road by learning through trial and error. Moving to a country not knowing the native language, overcoming stereotypes as a minority, and becoming self-made are all journeys on the hard road. There was no other way to describe the beginning of my career.

I was a new face and nameless in the professional boxing world. There were no big names, sponsors, or promoters backing me. I didn't have the opportunity to test the market because my rights were unlawfully signed away to Tee for a certain number of fights and years. Any young boxer could have looked at my business ordeal and quit, then moved on to something else.

Quitting was never an option or thought. Adversity is a part of any journey, regardless of which route you choose. Having a long-term vision blinded me from my short-term obstacles. I couldn't accomplish what I came to do in the boxing world during my first contract. I planned on running through every opponent standing in my way and positioning myself to get compensated top dollar for my boxing gifts.

My primary source of income during the early stages of my pro career was my job as a personal trainer at LA Fitness. Ironically, it was the same LA Fitness I got arrested in front of. Helping clients improve their health gave me another sense of fulfillment while enduring the toughest stint of my boxing career. I spoke my favorite job into existence by telling a friend who used to sneak me into the gym that I would become a personal trainer there one day. Helping clients improve their health was my only focus until I began training Marcia. Connecting with my clients became a primary purpose after she and I became friends.

My friendship with Marcia made me realize that relationships are a currency. A customer would pay the gym $100 for a session, but I'd only get paid less than 10%. Marcia made sure 70% went into my pockets. After a few months of training her and her husband at LA Fitness, they invited me to start training them at their house. I began feeling like we were related after visiting their residence a few times, but that feeling intensified once I met their family.

Marcia and her husband, Marc, moved to Houston from their native country, Brazil, shortly before I began training them. One of the things I loved about Marcia the most was her confidence in me. When I spoke about my dreams to her, she believed in them while they were still a vision. Her support and willingness to look out for me deepened our bond.

Marcia did many great things for me, but the best thing she ever did for me was introduce me to her niece, Raquel. I didn't speak a lick of Portuguese, and she didn't speak a lick of English, but her vibe was something I never felt before, and I wanted to explore it further. Our first few interactions went under her family's radar, but her blushes and my grins couldn't be disguised.

When she left for Brazil, a piece of me went with her. We weren't in a relationship, but my feelings were so strong for her that I would joke around with other people and tell them my girlfriend was in Brazil. Since childhood, I envisioned marrying a Brazilian woman. Your subconscious is the most fruitful place to plant something.

I knew what I envisioned for a wife, but my family didn't. Several months after Raquel's visit, I discovered that she could only return under certain stipulations. Being married was one of them.

My family didn't know how I felt about Raquel at that point. She felt like the potential woman of my dreams, but during that timeframe, they saw her as a girl I barely knew. At that age, she was still learning herself, but I had confidence about the woman she would evolve into.

Marcia told me to give it some time to decide if I wanted to marry her, but I didn't need much. My mind was already made up. We were at a justice of peace exchanging vows before anyone in my family knew about it.

Sometimes, it's best to keep certain blessings to ourselves. I wanted to stand on my own decision without any outside influences. I did what worked best for us and no one else.

If I had the opportunity to turn back the hands of time, I would play it the exact same way. My family didn't know about our marriage for months. It might have been longer if it wasn't for social media.

Shortly after Raquel changed her last name on Facebook, my mom called to ask me about it. Hours later, I gathered with my mom, dad, sister, and other family members to ask them if they thought I should marry Raquel.

Most of my family and friends thought I lost my mind, but I felt otherwise. My fantasy had already materialized. My dad calmly discussed it with me and trusted me to make the right decision. It took everything in me to keep a straight face while I asked them a question I already answered. She was already Mrs. Prograis and the woman I wanted to spend the rest of my life with.

There are hard roads in relationships, but all of them aren't the same. Each couple faces unique challenges and battles. Raquel and I faced unforeseen obstacles, but I never imagined connecting with someone so deeply. We were taking a chance on each other. We hadn't spent years together or seen how each other acts when mad. Also, there were linguistic challenges. Regardless of the obstacles in our way, we vowed to overcome them together. The most underrated aspect of the hard road is the end reward. It's easy to forget how fruitful the rewards will be while you are getting it out of the mud, but a seed only blossoms after it's covered in dirt.

Sometimes, when we aren't where we want to be, we should ask God why we are there. Aside from paying the bills and impacting clients, I knew I was at LA Fitness for different reasons. I was there to find my wife, build relationships that will last a lifetime, and finance my dreams.

When I started at LA Fitness, a colleague told me that many of our clients would become family. I didn't believe him at first, but he prophesized something. Picking up reading was another deep reason why I was at LA Fitness.

Books became the secret weapon for accelerating my personal life and career. Reading books about legends taught me intimate details about their lives, such as their pitfalls, adversities, mindsets, and families. I pulled from numerous boxing books to help me develop as a boxer and other genres of books to help me evolve as a man and entrepreneur.

. . .

Boxing can get political, but what aspect of life isn't? Politics is at the root of our society, ranging from government to novice sports. Relationships play a major factor in politics. Boxing politics often boils down to who you know. A good manager has business relationships with matchmakers, TV networks, and promoters that will help make the boxer become a moneymaker for all parties involved.

Tee didn't have any major connections in the boxing world, but I believed in him and everything he told me. He told me I would be a star soon, and my wife felt the same way. At the time, she worked at a Brazilian steakhouse, and I had yet to make any significant money from boxing.

During one stint, Raquel paid most of the bills. I was only responsible for putting food on the table, which was a struggle for me at times. Every time I think about Raquel's sacrifices, I fall deeper in love with her.

Raquel's employer unethically took capitalism to another level. He owned a restaurant in a popular part of town. All his workers were from different countries, some were legal citizens, and others weren't. Either way, he paid them under the table. My wife earned $25 for an 8-hour shift on weekdays.

On weekends, she earned $50 for 12-hour shifts. Some days, she came home more worn out than me. The fact that we were able to enjoy our time together while we were busting our asses and barely getting compensated for it shows the depth of our love.

When opportunities don't come our way, we have to create them. I did that for boxing and my job as a personal trainer. My clientele became stagnant, but I didn't complain or accept the circumstances. I printed 100 fliers and put them in mailboxes throughout Marcia's neighborhood. Only two people called me, but those clients helped me make ends meet and showed me that the extra mile is always worth it.

Tee went the extra mile to start my pro career. He organized a boxing event at an elementary school cafeteria in my neighborhood. It took several months to find my first pro opponent. Therefore, I was more concerned about getting my feet wet than where I fought.

I was compensated a $600 check for my first fight, but I knew I wasn't getting paid for my second bout before I stepped into the ring. It was my responsibility to sell the tickets and pay my opponent. I sold $3,000 worth of tickets, but that's how much I had to pay the person I'd be fighting. This is one of the downfalls of not having a promoter or high-level manager.

My opponent, Aaron Anderson, fought world champions, including Terence Crawford and Keith Thurman. Getting an opportunity to fight him was worth the sacrifice of potentially not making any money. Our match was in Texas City, Texas, and one of the first fights of the night on the undercard. I had the knockout of the night when I connected with a body shot that sounded over the crowd. It sounded like I sold $50,000 worth of tickets when I heard the crowd react.

Most boxers get asked for autographs after knocking someone out, but no one asked me for an autograph that night. While looking at pictures from this fight during this book's creation process, I quickly figured out why. I wasn't dressed like a professional boxer who just knocked someone out. I was dressed like I was going paintballing or leaving the house to run

136

errands with the hopes of no one seeing me. Meanwhile, Raquel was dressed like the wife of a boxing champion. In an abundance of ways, she was instrumental to my growth.

The dynamics of our household shifted once Raquel stormed through the door one hour after her shift started on a Friday afternoon. I was about to nap, but I was fully awake after hearing her cries when she entered the apartment. Things were always jacked up at that restaurant, but things reached a breaking point when Raquel quit. While she wept on my chest, I knew I had to put my family on my back, so my wife wasn't subject to situations like this.

The sun always finds a way to shine through storms in my life. The following week after my wife quit, I landed a sponsor and several new training clients and secured a profitable fight. Things were falling into place, but everyone in my corner wouldn't rejoin us for the next fight.

The most substantial advantages in life
are mental, not physical.

———————

LESSON

CHAPTER 16

My Corner

Who is in your corner? That's a question everyone must ask themselves. They can lead you to your goals, downfall, or mediocrity. What are the roles of the people in your corner? Is friend #1 the one you do business with? Is friend #2 the person you can confide in? Is friend #3 the one you can't tell anything to because they can't hold water? Your corner can quickly lead to your demise if people don't know their roles.

For example, a conversation about a business idea would be productive if you had a group discussion with friends #1 and #2. Talking about that with friend #3 could lead to chaos.

The higher your goals, the tighter-knit your team should be. Hidden agendas shouldn't be a part of the plan. Everyone should be willing to sacrifice to achieve the ultimate goal.

If not, people will begin taking up space and holding you back. Sometimes, we have to ask ourselves if a relationship is worth our progress. On occasion, it may be, but that's not always the case. Many people never reach their full potential because of their corner.

A culture in my corner began cultivating once I added a new element to my training. In one of the least expected moments, a familiar face became an asset and member of my team.

A friend and I were half-assing at a track after training on a Saturday morning. While we joked around, a commanding voice yelled, "Aye! Aye! Y'all are disrespecting my sport running like that."

While he powerwalked in our direction, I didn't know if I should laugh or take him seriously. Our introduction was a prelude to our relationship. Before we could answer, he squinted his eyes and asked, "Where do I know y'all from?"

When we realized we knew each other from Savannah Gym, he continued, "Yeah, yeah, that's right! I was Juan Diaz's bodyguard. I've seen you two before. I was a track star before this, and I can help y'all with strength and conditioning. All great boxers are great runners, and that wasn't no great running I just witnessed y'all doing."

Stopping what he was doing to provide us with valuable knowledge when he didn't know what he would get in return was enough for me to accept his offer. I instantly saw the value he added. Aside from pushing my mental and physical strength to new heights, Evins Tobler, my new strength & conditioning coach, added a perfect blend of personality to my corner and made my grind more enjoyable.

Initially, I didn't see the need for a strength and conditioning coach. I was a certified personal trainer and could have easily said, "I can do this by myself." Many people rob themselves of success by trying to do it independently and taking the proverbial self-made route. Having someone with specialized expertise in your corner will help expedite your growth.

The most important role to know in your corner is your own. Are you the golden goose, patriarch, or matriarch in your family? Are people counting on you to make it and help others make it out? Is someone close to you that person? Michael Jackson would have had a tougher route to becoming the legend he was if there were no Tito, Jermaine, Marlon, and Jackie.

If your corner can get on one accord, your chances of success increase. I attribute so much of my success to my corner, but I gradually built it. A pre-requisite for anyone in your corner should be belief in the main mission.

It would be debilitating if a talented businesswoman dreamed of building a business empire and her spouse didn't believe in her. Imagine a musician playing his mixtape for a woman, and she tells him it's the worst thing she ever heard. Everything isn't for everybody, but if the people in your corner don't believe in your mission, you'll have a harder time achieving it, and you should re-evaluate your support system.

The most substantial advantages in life are mental, not physical. If you don't believe in the work you put in, then you are conning yourself and working toward nothing. Your mind must be a part of your grind. Turning pro did something to my spirit and my mindset. I reassessed my growth and realized that a key part of my development was what I did outside the ring.

Many of the big-named prospects I trained with at Savannah flamed out by the beginning of my pro career. Learning from a lot of their downfalls helped me avoid having my own. I wouldn't have had that opportunity by remaining in New Orleans, where there wasn't a large community of amateur and professional boxers. My sacrifices and investments were beginning to surface.

A person in my corner showed me the importance of sacrificing immediate gratification. One of the biggest reasons a person would be willing to sacrifice is if they could see the vision of the end goal. Head boxing trainers typically get compensated 10% of the boxer's purses. There are no purses for amateur fighters, and purses for most pro boxers early in their career are typically small. On the other hand, once a boxer's career takes off, their trainer's compensation takes off simultaneously.

My trainer at the time overlooked my potential, so sacrificing for our careers to take off together didn't seem worth it to him. After my second professional bout, my trainer approached me about getting paid $100 a week for his services.

His unexpected switch-up caught me off guard. That was a lot of money for me to sacrifice at the time and against boxing protocols, but my father and I sacrificed to pay him for a month or so. Then, my manager and I decided we should go in a different direction for training. My trainer had a nonchalant attitude about us parting ways. That reinforced how much he valued and perceived me as a boxer. I was thankful for the time and effort he put into developing me, but I had burning ambitions to show him how successful I could become.

During the ring walk for my third fight, it looked like I was walking up the ramp of the Superdome to watch a New Orleans Saints game. Tee stepped in as my trainer for my third fight, and convinced me that it would be a smart idea for us to walk to the ring wearing New Orleans Saints attire. When I pulled off my Saints gear, it felt like I was about to scrap with someone on the streets.

The interesting thing about grinding is that you never know when your time to blow up will come. In this era, we all are one click, conversation, achievement, or phone call away from blowing up. We must be prepared for that opportunity. Tee made me feel like my time was now after my third fight. He reiterated that I was about to be a star several times after I exited the ropes that night.

Tee had the ability to make everything sound good and could have been one of the best salesmen on the planet. He made me feel like life was bound to take off at any moment. I took his words literally and decided it was the perfect timing for Raquel and me to officially add to our family.

Despite my wife being in between jobs, and me struggling financially, we knew the timing was right. That's how much we believed in us. I was more confident about our relationship than the timing of my come up.

Sometimes, our sacrifices are unknown even to the people around us. Most of my family and friends from New Orleans drove several hours to watch my fourth fight. Unfortunately, it was on the brink of not happening.

I did my part by weighing in at 140 pounds and grinding through training camp. Most boxers who have problems making weight are usually struggling to shed the final pounds. My opponent had a different type of problem making weight. He weighed in at 138lbs. - two pounds under the weight limit. Therefore, I had to lose two pounds in less than a day, or the fight was off. I was faced with a task that appeared impossible at the time, but I had to make it happen. My people had already sacrificed and traveled to see me, and I needed the money and opportunity.

I ran on a treadmill wearing a sauna suit, multiple layers, and boots while spitting as much as possible for an hour. My jaws were sucked in, and I felt like skin and bones, but I still had to put on a show. I got the knockout in the second round by delivering a body shot the audience and my opponent will remember for a lifetime.

After the fight, I felt anger that I'll remember for a lifetime. When I approached Tee about getting paid, he told me that couldn't happen because I didn't sell enough tickets.

Tee's ability to smooth things over after I didn't get paid spoke volumes about his sales skills. He quickly had me refocused on the big picture. The dust was still settling in my corner. Tee was capable of training me, but he functioned better as my manager.

Our personalities clashed, and that isn't an ideal dynamic between a boxer and head trainer. Tee and I had the same birthday and similarities, but most of our friction came from him treating me the same at 17 and 22. It was ok for him to embarrass me in front of others when I was younger, but I grew out of accepting that as I got older.

The deeper issue was how he communicated with me in the ring. Tee motivated me and was a great trainer, but when it was time for direction, he would shout with limited practical advice. He wasn't as technical as my first trainer in the pros. If I went through a round of exchanges with my opponent, Tee would yell, "Hit him and stop letting him hit you!"

On the contrary, my first trainer would calmly say, "When he throws a left, sidestep him and hit him with a right hook."

Boxers and trainers always need to be in sync and communicate effectively. Tee and I were tight outside of the ring, but we would always be one sentence away from an argument when we were in the ring. We decided it was best that he stuck to managing me and started looking for a trainer.

Having what you don't want helps you figure out what you want. My first trainer and I had a productive relationship. I appreciated the time he spent training me, but our disconnect helped me define what I wanted and didn't want in a boxing coach.

I needed specialized attention and someone who believed in me. My next trainer would have a different set of unexpected qualities. When I got the news that I would be training with a former Olympic Medalist, I couldn't have been more thrilled. My new trainer was close friends with Pernell Whitaker, a Hall-of-Fame boxer I idolize.

When I arrived at the gym to train with him for the first time, I felt like a kid on the first day of school. He appeared to be excited as well when we first met. After we shook hands, he pointed me toward the speedbag and told me to start there. Before I threw my first punch, he was sitting on the couch near the entrance.

Once I approached him after I finished, he kept his head in his phone and pointed for me to do another drill. For a minute, I began feeling like the grass wasn't greener on the other side. I always wanted my first trainer to give me more attention, but my second trainer gave me even less. He was very knowledgeable, but only shared a little bit of his knowledge with me.

My first fight after starting to train with him was on the outskirts of New Orleans. The neighboring parish was my first dose of fighting back home as a pro. Fighting in a small setting gave me aspirations of performing on a big stage back home.

The hotel audience of a few hundred people was filled with close friends and family members. I pulled up to the fight in my truck, but I imagined being driven in a limo and escorted into an arena. My nerves were the last thing on my mind when I arrived at my first pro fight back home. That morning, I had breakfast at IHOP, and food poisoning took over my body before leaving the restaurant.

My fifth pro fight was a shitty situation. I used the bathroom six times and threw up twice before the fight. Things got so bad that I used the restroom after my hands were wrapped. I did everything possible to avoid getting my wraps dirty, but I am not sure I succeeded.

My opponent, Adauto Gonzalez, was a Mexican boxer reminiscent of many boxers I fought in Houston. Mexican boxers are known for coming to fight and slugging it out to the end. That's what my rugged opponent and I did. Thankfully, he did not punch me in the stomach.

I hit him with everything in the book, but didn't have my normal power behind it because of food poisoning. This victory showed me that I have to be ready for any obstacle thrown at me leading up to a fight and during it.

Four months later, I returned home for another match in the metropolitan area. A new era of New Orleans boxing was emerging during my sixth fight. My fight at the Gretna Festival was staged in a neighborhood park. This match was more than just another day at the office. My friends had been bragging about me, but I was still grouped with other local boxers besides Marcus McDaniel. He was the only other one who made a name for himself outside of the city at the time.

I was matched up with a local boxer and had to lose 12 pounds in two days, or the fight would be off. Despite the hectic weight cut, I put on a great performance. However, I didn't leave the ring unscathed. A few punches to the ear caused the cartilage to inflame.

My ear was in pain, but it wasn't a big deal to me because it's a typical injury in all combat sports. However, my grandmother thought it was the end of the world. She thought I could die from it and begged me to go to the hospital. As I denied her requests, she questioned if I should stop boxing. To ease her mind, I went to the doctor with her.

The physician didn't know what to do with the cauliflower ear, but I still had to pay him. The bill was the same amount as my profit for the fight, and I fixed my ear the next day. I was back broke again, but I had to keep pushing.

My second trainer and I parted ways after my 6th fight. He was an expert and enjoyable to work with, but I needed someone more hands-on. I realized that my growth would be my responsibility. If I lost that fight because I depended on my trainer to show me the way, it would be my fault, not his.

When I ran miles before the sun came up in high school, I wondered what the difference was between putting in work early in the morning versus the evening time. The crowd at the track was nearly empty before daybreak, but crowded in the evening. There are debates about which time of the day is best to work out. The undebatable aspect about running before daybreak is that it gives you a head start on the day and your competition.

Aspirations to become my best had me up grinding before daybreak. Sometimes, I wondered if it was worth getting up that early to work out in the morning. Going the extra mile led me to a career-changing partnership and life-changing relationship.

149

Never underestimate the impact of a first impression. Bobby Benton first saw me when I was 17, running at Memorial Park before daybreak. We became familiar faces because he would be out there training his boxers at the same time. In his eyes, I set myself apart from other fighters before he knew me because I was always willing to make the sacrifices others weren't. I knew the same thing about Bobby and that we paired together perfectly.

Bobby was born into boxing, and his father owned Heights Gym, a legendary staple in Houston. A long list of world champions trained there. Bobby's dad wore almost every hat in the boxing world, including trainer, manager, boxing gym owner, and matchmaker, along with other roles. He encouraged his son to take a different path, but Bobby fell in love with boxing at a young age. His passion for the sport led him to begin training amateur boxers at 18 and opening Mainstreet Boxing Gym.

My corner evolved into a family environment. Bobby contributed to that sentiment by showing up at the hospital when my son Ray was born. Watching him develop during my wife's pregnancy was one of the most fulfilling times in my life. I still remember the first time I felt his kicks and punches in Raquel's stomach. His emergence gave my world greater meaning.

I was now responsible for life's greatest blessing and gave life to someone more meaningful than myself. When I held my son for the first time, a fire was ignited in me to become the best man I could be. My heart was overpouring with love, but my face didn't show it. I felt like I let myself and my family down.

While growing up, I visualized being rich or financially stable when my first child was born. However, I only had a couple hundred dollars to my name at the time. I felt some type of way about myself, and the look on my face was evident from pictures taken that day. I experienced the ultimate joy inside when my son, Ray Prograis, was born on October 20, 2013, but it was hard for me to show it because I couldn't provide my firstborn with the life I envisioned for him.

While Bobby prepared to leave the hospital, he told me to call him in a few weeks when I was ready to start back training. I told him I'd be ready in a few hours. St. Joseph's Hospital, where Ray was born, is three blocks away from Bobby's gym. Bobby met me at the gym late that night and showed me that he was willing to go the extra mile for me, my family, and my career.

Before then, I didn't think I could be more motivated, but walking out of the hospital with Ray and Raquel took my motivation to new levels. It was one thing to let myself down, but feeling like I let my family down was something deeper. I felt a greater sense of urgency to make it because I was officially responsible for leading a family.

Having Ray under my wings made me want to be the epitome of a man and provider. My first taste of leading a family happened when my mother moved out, but this was more responsibility. Ray's birth instantly made me take things to the next level.

There will always be distractions,
but there won't always be opportunities.

———————

LESSON

CHAPTER 17

New Levels

Deciphering if something is beneficial for us is a constant decision we must make throughout our lives. That ranges from environments to relationships, what we consume, and how we express our emotions. During one of my first fights, I learned the balance between healthy and unhealthy inspiration.

Inspiration is usually the start of every dream. When I was a kid, Mike Tyson, Allen Iverson, and Kobe Bryant were three of my biggest athletic inspirations. Imitating Iverson and Kobe wouldn't have taken me as far as imitating Tyson. I wouldn't have been able to inspire people worldwide, make millions, accomplish history, and perform across the world if I decided to stick with basketball and draw from an unhealthy inspiration.

Healthy inspiration almost became unhealthy leading up to one of my first pro fights. At the time, I was watching a lot of film on Oscar De La Hoya. During sparring, I would hold my hands like him and use some of his moves. Training camp and sparring sessions are usually when I try imitating other boxing legends. This time, I tried mimicking one in an official match.

Because of that, shit got real when it didn't have to during the fight.

You can try to be someone else all you want, but shit hits the fan when you get in a situation that only the person you are emulating knows how to get out of. I had to start being Regis Prograis to turn things around and get the victory.

Not having a concrete identity made me reflect on my amateur days when I was being talked about while sparring. I had a ponytail at the time, and two old heads were standing ringside. As I was in the mix with another boxer, one of the men condescendingly asked, "Who does he think he is with that ponytail?"

The other man responded, "He doesn't know who he is yet."

Discovering who we truly are requires a soul-searching journey, but the faster we discover who we are, the quicker we can fulfill our life purposes and provide value to the world. Regardless of how much someone inspires us, it is essential to carve our own paths. Muhammad Ali inspired me more than any other boxer, but I wouldn't use his defensive style of leaning back during a fight or shuffling my feet to entertain the crowd and throw off my opponent. If I strayed away from what works for me to emulate his style, I wouldn't have been able to etch my own path in boxing history.

Expenses were piling up, but the boxing and LA Fitness checks weren't. Fighting for free, being underpaid, signed to a bad contract, and family dynamics were a lot to keep off my mind while ascending through the ranks. The adversity and responsibilities increased my motivation and deepened my focus.

There will always be distractions, but there won't always be opportunities. Regardless of which challenges came my way, they never came before boxing.

Before I became a parent, I heard other people my age talk about how a serious relationship and having a kid would set them back. Starting a family increased my sense of urgency for success, and it showed in the ring.

Fatherhood helped turn a friendship into a brotherhood. Benji and I were becoming fathers simultaneously. He was 16 at the time, but more mature than most grown men. A lot can be said about a person's character based on how they react to unforeseen situations.

Benji was a high school football star who scored four touchdowns in one half during his freshman year, and a talented musician. As a teenager, he stood up like a real man should after finding out he had a child on the way. Benji prioritized his family to become the father he never had. We shared a sense of urgency to make it for our families. Once we reconnected, he became an important part of my corner and was willing to play any role to help us make it.

The foundation of my team was finally coming together. None of us believed in shortcuts and we knew the hard road was the only route to our destination. Searching for the easy route will take you down the wrong road. Choosing the hard route in the gym expedited my progress. I identified my toughest sparring test shortly after finding my gym home.

Austin Trout was one of the people I looked up to the most at Main Street Gym. His journey impacted me deeply because I watched him graduate from contender to world champion, and he co-signed me during a humbling moment. Months before our most impactful interaction, he became a star by defeating Hall-of-Fame boxer Miguel Cotto at Madison Square Garden in front of 1,000,000 viewers.

We were at two different stages in our careers, but I was eager to spar with him. He just had a close fight with Canelo Alvarez and was in training camp for a bout with Erislandy Lara. I was a prospect preparing for my seventh fight and convinced Bobby to let me spar with him.

I was still a new face in the gym, so I caught him by surprise on our first day of sparring. My desire to prove myself against a big name set the tone for my productive day. The following day, Austin set the tone for how I would approach sparring for years to come.

He countered all the moves I hit him with the day before, and I left the ring with black eyes. I felt humbled when I exited the ropes, but he lifted me to new heights shortly after. While I was doing an interview after sparring, Austin put his arms around me and proudly proclaimed that I would be the next world champion out of Main Street Boxing Gym.

...

Boxing is one of the hardest sports to break into. There aren't any colleges grooming you to become a productive part of the workforce or economy. Many college athletes have their education to fall back on if they don't proceed to the next level athletically. Boxers don't have any systematic backup plans that college institutions provide student-athletes. My team and I were taking a chance on each other with no backup plans. We were at the bottom, but didn't consider any alternative routes if boxing didn't work out.

My first fight with Bobby was in the capital of my home state. The Belle of Baton Rouge was one of the best promotional events I fought in during the early stages of my career. That didn't mean I wouldn't experience friction there. My reputation in Louisiana climbed after my previous two fights. That caused my initial opponent to duck me and fight someone else on the card.

The person who ducked me would be fighting someone else from Louisiana, who had a bone to pick with me. He had just served time in Angola Penitentiary, one of the roughest prisons in the country, where most inmates are serving life sentences.

We were in the same weight division and had a rivalry I didn't know about until he started mugging me at weigh-ins. Bobby asked if I had a problem with him. I didn't, but apparently, he had a problem with me. Our problem ended after he approached me post-fight.

My performance earned everyone's respect that night. We shook hands and left our problems at the weigh-in. Crossing paths with him showed me that the ring is the best place to earn my counterpart's respect.

Bobby and I drove from Houston to Monroe, Louisiana, for what was supposed to be our second fight together. Taking the back roads to northern Louisiana to fight in a small venue symbolized the hard road we faced. Streets with no street signs, bumps in the road, and loss of signal correlated with our long and short-term destinations. I was drained from cutting weight, exhausted due to restless nights from parenting a newborn, and riding in a car for several hours, but I couldn't have been more ready to fight my opponent.

The motel where we stayed for the fight looked like a spot where a couple would get busted on the TV show Cheaters. Prostitution and drug deals were going on while we checked in. After we got settled in the room, Bobby's phone began blowing up. His face dropped once the person on the other end began speaking. I didn't think much of it until he told me the fight was canceled, and my opponent wasn't showing up.

This was supposed to be my eighth professional fight. I had career earnings of a few thousand dollars and didn't expect to earn much for that fight, but a win that day would have moved me closer to bigger paydays. Instead, Bobby and I took a loss from having to spend money and time preparing for a night that was called off at the last minute.

I didn't dwell on the anger because Bobby still found a way for us to enjoy the trip. We watched the other fights on the card, went to mom-and-pop shops in town, and watched VHS tapes on the 20-inch TV in the motel.

Struggling to make weight and make ends meet led me to compete in the 147-pound division for the first time. I wanted to get it on as much as possible during this stage of my career. I knew I was taking a chance when I watched film of my opponent knocking several people out. He was a power puncher, and my power would be tested during my 8th pro fight. I passed the test when I stopped my opposition 15 seconds into the sixth round.

The urgency to get my name out there heightened after another fight fell through in north Louisiana. Bobby and I drove to Shreveport, Louisiana for a fight, and it was canceled last minute again. While I was stretched out in the motel, I didn't think things could get more upsetting. However, a new nerve was struck when the entire card fell through.

We couldn't even be entertained after we were scheduled to do the entertaining. The promoters of the fight ghosted everyone after everything was called off. Unfortunately, my troubles didn't stop there.

Imagine clocking in at work and being paid a different wage from what you agreed to work for. After my 9th fight, I approached the promoter for my paycheck. Tee was out of town during this fight, but the promoter told me to call him for my payment. When Tee told me to call the promoter back, he explained that I only sold $1,900 worth of tickets, and had to cross the threshold of $2,000 to earn payment for the fight.

I was still responsible for paying Bobby, Evins, and other expenses. I felt like anything but a boss at that moment and realized how important it was for me to become one. My talent was responsible for feeding my family and paying my corner. Becoming a world champion would put me in the position to bless so many people, but I had to become a boss inside and outside the ring to make that happen.

I'll never forget that ride back from Mississippi with my father. I vented to him the entire ride. My emotions were running high, but my dad's wise words and calm demeanor helped me keep a cool head. We began thinking of ways to get my name out there, and that topic became a focal point in my corner.

It's no one else's responsibility to put you
on, aside from yourself. How a person gets
on is a testament to their testimony.

———————

LESSON

CHAPTER 18

Rougarou

Being a prize fighter and world champion is a job inside and outside the ring. When you think of Muhammad Ali, Floyd Mayweather, Mike Tyson, both Sugar Rays, and Oscar De La Hoya, a persona comes to mind, along with their boxing skills. Non-boxing fans will tune in to see them lose, cheer them on, or say they watched the fight because it is a trending topic in society.

Would Ali be as famous of a fighter if he didn't have a poetic, prophetic, and comical speech before every fight? Would Oscar De La Hoya or both Sugar Rays be as popular if they weren't articulate charmers made for the spotlight? Would these Hall-of-Fame boxers be as famous without their larger-than-life personalities? They would be to me, but the world outside of boxing wouldn't have appreciated their boxing skills as much if it wasn't for their showmanship.

One of the best ways for fighters to build their brand and connect with fans is to have an alter ego. My team and I knew I needed one. One day after training, my dad, Tee, and Bobby were sitting ringside. Taking my brand to new levels was on everybody's mind after I was performing like a star in the ring but neglected on the business side of things. My corner and I knew we were underachieving in that department.

While we sat ringside, Bobby asked, "What are we going to do about a nickname for Regis?" Everyone exchanged glances in silence. While no one could come up with a name, he suggested, "How about Rifle Regis Prograis?"

We laughed and collectively answered, "No!"

"Crescent City Crusher?" Tee suggested.

My dad responded, "Nah, that sounds like a heavyweight. That name won't fit him."

Tee followed up, "New Orleans Nightmare! That's it!"

We all agreed that wasn't it as soon as he suggested it. I thought we hit a dead end until my dad shouted, "Rougarou! Regis Rougarou Prograis!"

It sounded good when he proudly said it, but I didn't know what it was. Tee clapped, then pointed at my dad and said, "That's it! That's it! Regis Rougarou Prograis."

My nickname and boxing alter ego became an aggressive and dangerous dog-headed magical monster from the swamps of Louisiana. The moniker grew on me because it flowed perfectly with my biological name, represented my home, and signified the dog and magic within me. My style and brand graduated during my 10th fight. I always wanted to come out like Mike Tyson during my ring walk. He used to enter the ring shirtless and with a face of terror.

Before the fight, my father designed a Rougarou mask for me. The crowd at the Athletic Fencing Center in Houston gave me an applause like never before when I walked out to the ring in the mask he made. I felt the energy of Tyson flowing through my veins also because I walked into the ring shirtless like him. The fans were entertained before my fight started, but I gave them an even better show once the event began.

The beginning of the fight started like a one-sided hockey fight. I began beating my opponent and walking him down shortly after the bell rang for the first round. Almost every punch I landed in the ring that was prompted on a platform in the middle of a ballroom generated an ooh or ah from the audience.

The chants from the crowd drowned out my opponent's groans and remarks in the audience. I didn't hear any of it until Marco shouted, "Knock him out his britches Regis!" After my friend's joke, the crowd could have easily been mistaken for a comedy show audience. Laughing was the last thing on my mind. I was ready to give the crowd what they came for, but the ref paused the action because my opponent's trunks came off.

He received one of the worst tape jobs I ever saw. His corner wrapped white bandages around the waist of his trunks, then he trotted back to the middle of the ring for the last few seconds of the first round. He was saved by the shorts momentarily.

Once the second round started, I hit my opponent with several jabs, then a five-punch combination that ended with a left hook that put him on his back. The crowd thought he was okay to continue because he got up quickly, but that isn't an indicator a fighter is fine. I knew he was done before I dropped him, but he made the count.

After the ref tried to continue the fight, the other corner got the ref's attention and waved the white flag. My opponent pleaded to his corner and the ref to let us continue, but they saved him from himself. The crowd started booing when the ref stopped the fight, but they began cheering again after I was announced as the winner.

Knowing when to stop a fight is one of the most intricate areas of boxing. The stoppage of fights has caused riots, lifelong debates, and career-ending losses. Not stopping them in time has caused deaths. There is a long list of fighters who didn't live to fight another day because their fight wasn't stopped soon enough. Money is often prioritized before the fighter's well-being by spectators and sometimes even their own corner.

Corners play the most important role in knowing when to stop a fight. They should know when their fighter can't come back or if they are unfit to continue. My opponent's corner recognized something the audience didn't. When I went to his locker room after the fight to show my sportsmanship, he didn't know who I was or where he was.

I began feeling the impact of my alter-ego immediately after the fight. Minutes before leaving the venue, I was interviewed by a media outlet. One of their questions was about my mask, and they used a picture of me in it to market our interview. I was happy about the progress, but still upset about some of my challenges and adversities.

People were in my ear about their lack of belief in Tee as a manager, but I respected his hustle to the fullest, and he had some innovative ideas. Sometimes, ideas remain idle when a person doesn't have connections to the right people. Nonetheless, Tee did what he could and found ways to make things happen from time to time.

He entered the boxing game by getting on with trainer Ronnie Shields. It's no one else's responsibility to put you on, aside from yourself. How a person gets on is a testament to their testimony. He volunteered to help Ronnie for free. Many people turn their noses up at free opportunities, but sometimes, that's the best way to expedite your growth and get your feet wet.

Tee learned Spanish on his own and could speak it conversationally. That made him a valuable asset to Ronnie, who had a lot of Spanish boxers and no one to communicate with them until Tee came along. He also helped make my career enjoyable because of the friendship we developed. A spontaneous and unprecedented move was one of his most impactful contributions to my career.

My manager and I still felt uneasy about the fights falling through in north Louisiana. We knew that wouldn't have happened with a high-level boxing promoter. A few weeks after my fight was canceled, he asked me to meet him at Cane's.

We had some small talk, but I could tell something was on his mind. When I asked him if he was ok while we waited for our food, he said, "Let me see your phone." Then handed it back and said, check your tweets.

Tee tweeted promoter Lou DiBella from my account and said, "I am a 10-0 fighter based out of Houston, Texas. I knocked out eight of my first ten opponents, and I am ready to take my career to the next level."

Lou DiBella, the former HBO Sports Vice President, had seen everything in boxing. When Tee reached out to him, we both saw something new. I don't know if anyone else in boxing history ever secured a contract via Twitter, but it worked for me.

Lou began promoting me starting with my 12th fight. He brought some structure and stability to my career. Each fight had a minimum amount of how much I would earn. The days of fighting for free were officially over. I will always be thankful for Lou because no other promoters were willing to take a chance on me. I was compensated $3,500 for my first fight with him, which was a significant step toward bigger paydays.

Remaining disciplined while experiencing
more freedom is a test of willpower and how
badly we want to accomplish our goals.

———————

LESSON

CHAPTER 19

ShoBox

S tep-up fights are opportunities for promotions in the boxing world. Step-up fights can change a fighter's life overnight. Before Muhammad Ali's step-up fight against Sonny Liston, Ali was seen as an underdog and a top contender. Liston, the heavyweight champion at the time, was viewed as the most intimidating man in boxing. Ali's victory against Sonny changed their careers and perceptions overnight.

Step-up fights are usually planned, but one of mine happened unexpectedly. I only had a few days to prepare, which equates to no time for preparation in boxing. My 13th fight was supposed to be against a boxing prospect from another country with a record of 8 - 2.

There are plenty of boxing stars from countries outside the US, but not having any fighting experience in the US usually means they are less battle-tested. He didn't stand a chance against me. Although it seemed like a competitive fight on paper, my opponent dropped out at the last minute. The beautiful thing about working with a professional promoter was that he had the ability to fix things if something went wrong. Lou DiBella found a replacement quickly.

My opponent went from a prospect soon to be out of boxing to Hector Velasquez. He amassed 56 wins, fought Manny Pacquiao, competed in three weight classes, and made his pro debut when I was in pre-k. None of my opponents before this point had more than 20 fights in their careers. His experience and pedigree made him a step up in competition.

Our fight was scheduled for January 9, 2015, in California. At the turn of 2015, Floyd Mayweather and Manny Pacquiao were still champions and months away from their mega fight. I was still a prospect trying to make a name for myself and become a contender.

Experience is one of the most essential aspects of any craft. Boxers of my opponent's caliber have seen everything in the sport, including upsets, comebacks, victories, and world-class opponents. Hector Velasquez and I would be fighting on the undercard of a future opponent of mine, Ivan Redkach. That night, he won by stoppage in the 6th round. I had the second fight of the night after one of the funniest nicknames I ever heard in boxing. Derrick "Whup Dat Ass" Murray was scheduled to fight in the opening bout.

Dictating the fight against a reputable opponent who had been boxing pro since I was in pre-school boosted my confidence. I knew Bobby had faith in me, but I saw him get nervous for the first time when we got the news of who my replacement opponent would be. I showed him that there was no reason to worry about me when I stepped through the ropes.

Velasquez used his experience to survive until the fifth round, when we exchanged blows, and I landed a right cross that brutally ended the fight. My bout against the crafty veteran was my first pro fight outside of Louisiana, Texas, and Mississippi. A taste of California for the first time made me want to stay. Going from the sunny, cloudless sky in California to a gloomy, cold winter day in Texas made me think harder about what life would be like to live in California.

…

After knocking out my next opponent in less than two minutes, I earned another step-up fight. This would be my first televised fight and I'd be earning the biggest check at that point of my career. Nonetheless, I was more excited about testing myself against an opponent I respected. My ShoBox and television debut was scheduled for August 7, 2015.

Every training camp had been the same until this one. My wife and son went to Brazil one week before camp started. Being a new father and husband made me forget what me-time felt like. The silence in the apartment was loud when they left.

I took advantage of the alone time by shadowboxing, putting in extra work, and studying my craft. Remaining disciplined while experiencing more freedom is a test of willpower and how badly we want to accomplish our goals.

Boxing consumed all the downtime that I usually gave to my family. Grinding while they were away brightened our future.

Every day, I'd pick up something new and try it at the gym. One week before the fight, I felt more prepared than ever. Contrarily, I began feeling sicker than ever, but I was prepared for the obstacle. Showing the world the fighter I was becoming suppressed my thoughts of sickness.

Amos Cowart was a different breed from the opponents I faced until this point in my career. We fought on the same card during my previous fight in Connecticut. While I watched him dispatch his opponent in 5 rounds, I told Tee I wanted to fight him.

There are two types of boxers when it comes to climbing the boxing hierarchy - predators and scavengers. Predators hunt stronger opponents to build their skills, and scavengers prey on weaker opponents.

I knew Cowart would be a challenging test. He was undefeated, had never been past the sixth round, and knocked out nine of his first ten opponents. Both of us entered the ring with knockout power, mohawks, and ambitions to graduate from prospect to contender.

Cowart and I were scheduled for the night's first fight and didn't spend too much time feeling each other out in the opening rounds as most boxers do. I maintained a heightened sense of anticipation for his head-hunting punches. Fighters thirsting for the knockout excite the fans, but that is risky business against an effective counterpuncher.

Cowart tried to take my head off with almost every punch. That gave me the opportunity to make him miss and land numerous combinations. Punches were landed almost every few seconds of the fight.

Fighting him tested my endurance, chin, and ability to take body shots. He loaded up on most of his punches, but couldn't move me backward. The punches he threw took more out of him than me and robbed him of his steam.

We traded one punch for several on multiple occasions. His punches put 80% of his opponents down, but I powered through them, won unanimously, and broke a ShoBox record for most punches thrown in a fight. Overcoming the secret obstacle and having a vacation planned in Brazil after the fight made the victory even sweeter. Being able to celebrate outside the country made me hungry for the next obstacle to overcome.

When we are pushed to our limits, we have two options - accept our limitations or graduate to new levels.

———————

LESSON

CHAPTER 20

Recognition

Before my first TV fight, most of my vacations consisted of traveling back home to New Orleans. Going to Austin, Texas, as my first activity after the fight would have been fulfilling if that was all I had planned. However, that was only the first destination. Traveling out of the country for the first time to Brazil and having my son and wife there waiting for me did something to my spirit.

Stepping foot in a foreign land was more than I ever dreamed of. The air and ground felt different, but after getting acquainted, I was quickly reminded of how humanity is similar worldwide. Regardless of the similarities, I didn't know what anyone was saying. Context clues, reading body language and facial expressions, and my translator app were all I had to work with. Nonetheless, I enjoyed how the trip started.

After meeting the rest of Raquel's family, I was even more convinced we were meant to be. We all vibed, and they made me feel at home in a foreign place. On Saturday night during my first weekend, I decided to step out with her friends.

While we packed into a van, I was reminded of my AAU basketball days when we would ride in overcrowded vehicles to tournaments. The ride got even more uncomfortable ten minutes into the trip.

As we traveled on a dimly lit road, we were pulled over. A guy wearing an unbuttoned short-sleeved shirt forced us out of the van. When I smelled liquor on his breath and felt his aggression, I was prepared to defend myself, my wife, and the group. Curses were traded between my group and the badly dressed drunk while I watched in confusion.

Things appeared as if they were about to take a turn for the worse when the drunken man started recklessly waving a gun in our faces. When we became silent, he grinned, then tucked his firearm away in his waistband. All energy doesn't have to be matched. Fighting fire with fire could have led to a different outcome.

Escaping that situation had me on edge, but I was ready to party. I was always selective about my celebrations, and the occasion called for one that night, so I did my best to live in the moment. When I go out, I'm a fly on the wall mixed with a social butterfly. I feel out of the mix because I don't drink, and I am not much of a dancer, but I am good for a great convo in the club. Usually, I end up being someone a drunk person vents to. It's all fun and games when I'm not boxing, watching film, reading, or doing something to perfect my craft. After returning from bonding with Raquel's family and her country, working on my craft was the first thing on my mind.

My first title fight was in the same place as my fourth fight. The opportunity to earn a belt and headline an event in the city I evacuated to was a full-circle moment. I wasn't fighting for a world title, but it was a meaningful step in my career. This was another challenging test against my second undefeated fighter in a row. Seven of the eight prospects fighting that night were unbeaten, and our combined record was 92-1-5.

My opponent, Abel Ramos, was also signed with Lou DiBella and won the bronze medal at the 2010 US Boxing National Championships. The only blemishes on his record were two draws. Someone's 0 had to go in the loss column. We were scheduled to fight for the WBC–NABF Junior Light Welterweight Title on December 11, 2015, at the Bayou Event Center in Houston.

My performance in my previous bout led me from being the opening act to the closing one. I felt responsible for giving everyone a show worthy of being a headliner. Fighting in my second hometown gave me even more ammunition.

The confidence from dominating my previous opponent carried into my next fight. Abel Ramos's trash-talking had my grandmother concerned, but not me. She saw a clip of him saying how he would knock me out and asked me if I was sure

I wanted to fight him. Seeing something else on Instagram made me want to fight him even more.

My opponent was on social media doing donuts in a brand-new red Camaro. I wanted the same thing and felt like I deserved one too. Beating him would help me afford it. The circumstances around the fight made me anxious to step into the ring with him. When I saw Ramos at my gym leading up to the fight, I thought about confronting him, but I decided to save that energy for the ring.

I didn't take his words personally, but I fought him like I did. My defense that fight prompted an analyst to state that I showed shades of Pernell Whitaker. Pairing elusive defense with painful punches made it a rough night for my opponent. Ramos showed tremendous heart during the time we shared the ring. I splattered his blood across the ShoBox cameras, but he kept coming forward until his corner stopped the fight at the end of the 8th round.

Beating Ramos and winning my first belt in December symbolized my growth and the perfect way to end 2015. My first fight that year was my first time fighting outside of the southern region as a pro, and the beginning of a new level in my career. I entered the top 10 list of prospects in the 140-pound division and was selected as a "Prospect of The Year" by ESPN in 2015, along with Errol Spence Jr., Anthony Joshua, Oleksandr Usyk, Jose Ramirez, and other world-class fighters.

My next fight was the quickest professional victory of my career, but it wasn't an all-around win. Aaron Herrera and I were supposed to fight for the vacant WBC–USNBC Light-Welterweight title. I sat in the sauna for hours a day and ran outside in the Texas heat, but I was still heavier than I needed to be as training camp ended. I was pushed to my limits during training camp and trying to cut weight. When we are pushed to our limits, we have two options - accept our limitations or graduate to new levels.

One week leading up to the fight, when it felt like I had been pushed past my limit in the sauna, I found two more reasons to keep going. On this day, I did four 30-minute sessions in the sauna at LA Fitness. At this point, I began scaling back my work hours, so I was seen less by regulars at the gym.

Halfway into my last session in the sauna, a former client walked in. He was memorable because I helped him make a lifestyle change. My former client was 320 pounds when we met and making his last attempt at a fitness journey. Before we started training, he hated working out, but I made it fun for him. After one year of training him, he was almost down to 250 lbs. I spoke life into him and gave him positive energy when he needed it the most. His health was at the point where it began failing him.

When we caught up in the sauna, it had been two years since our last training session. His continuous weight loss made him hard to recognize. He vented about his lifestyle changes and fitness progress and then asked me what I had been up to.

Once I gave him an update on my boxing career, he suspiciously responded, "Aren't you too old to be trying to make it in boxing? I am surprised you are still fighting."

I've never been the defensive type to quickly get into my feelings. I casually responded, "Yeah, I'm still at it bro," and the conversation died right there.

His down talk gave me life. I felt like I couldn't go anymore in the sauna, but I pushed past my time limit. It was meant for me to remain in the sauna that day.

A few minutes after I was supposed to end the session, my former client began talking about how much he hated his job to the other people in the sauna. They all joined him on the soapbox. I didn't have any energy to participate, but that wasn't why I didn't join the convo.

I couldn't relate to their plights and wouldn't swap places with them for anything in the world. Even though I was going through an excruciating process of training camp and cutting weight, I was in love with boxing.

Being in love with something or someone means you are willing to accept the ups and downs. Trying your best at something and coming up short is a defeating feeling. I made extreme sacrifices to get down to 140 lbs., but I couldn't. Therefore, I wasn't eligible to fight for the belt. Regardless of how I performed in the ring, the winner of the Ivan Baranchyk and Nicholas Givan fight would take home a belt that was meant for me.

Tee was so mad that he didn't look in my direction until the fight was about to start. Bobby eased my mind by having an "oh well" reaction to it. Tee's reaction, my finances, misery from cutting weight, and missed opportunity gave me a sense of rage before the fight. I was ready to throw hands before I entered the ring that night.

My opponent was target practice for me, and I knocked him out 46 seconds after the fight started. I had already won the fight, but I wanted to fight some more after the 1st round knockout. I should have won my second belt two fights in a row once I dropped my opponent to the canvas with several body shots that I can still hear until this day. My frustration led me to get back in the gym the following week after I returned from Oklahoma.

There was no time to cry over spilled milk. My next fight would be on the biggest stage I fought on at that point in my career. Aside from my bouts on ShoBox, most of my first 17 fights were in small hotels or event centers.

My 18th fight would be at the Barclays Arena for the vacant WBC–USNBC Light-Welterweight title on June 25, 2016. The regional belt would be a significant step toward becoming a contender. Terence Crawford, Ricky Burns, and Julius Indongo were the world champions of my division at the time.

I was scheduled to fight on Shawn Porter and Keith Thurman's undercard. Thurman and Porter were top dogs in the 147-pound division, fighting for the WBA Welterweight world title. I was on the undercard for one of the biggest fights of 2016, but I had the mindset to steal the show. My name was reaching new heights, and this would be the perfect opportunity to get it out there even more so.

Throughout each stage of life, God showed me why I should trust His timing. Porter and Thurman were initially scheduled to fight on March 12, 2016, in Uncasville, Connecticut. That was two weeks before I faced Aaron Herrera. If Thurman wouldn't have been in a wreck one month before the initial fight date, I wouldn't have been able to be on the undercard. Also, their fight would have taken place on a smaller platform. Instead of the fight taking place in Uncasville, it would be in Brooklyn on one of the biggest boxing stages.

To make the spotlight even brighter, this was the first nationally televised boxing event since 1978, when Muhammad Ali fought Leon Spinks in the New Orleans Superdome. The historical event was a success. The card averaged 2.4 million viewers and generated $1.1 million in ticket sales, which was the highest gate in the history of Barclays Center to date. The onlookers would see one of the best knockouts of the year before one of the best fights of the year.

My taller opponent, Luis Florez, was coming off a defeat against former champion and military veteran Jamel Herring. Taller fighters are some of my favorite opponents because they are vulnerable to body shots. I used that to my advantage against Luis Florez during my 18th fight and the opportunity to win another championship belt.

I brought my game to the arena, but that was it. Boxing champions are known for arriving in style at the arena and press conferences, but I was dressed as if I snuck into the event.

Preparing for the unexpected is one of the best ways to take advantage of unforeseen opportunities. I looked like a champion in the ring, but didn't look like one outside the ring that night. While I watched Lou DiBella being interviewed at the press conference after the fight, a reporter mentioned my name. Once Lou began discussing me, I was invited on stage. I was thrilled when they asked me to come up, but I realized I wasn't prepared for the unexpected opportunity while walking up to the podium.

I was still on the rise, and many reporters there were just seeing me for the first time. Once professionals in the boxing world began saying my name, they would mispronounce it and mistake my ethnicity.

After I sat down, wearing a white t-shirt I purchased from a corner store in New Orleans, the first reporter started his first sentence in English. Then, he proceeded to ask me the rest of his questions in Spanish. The rest of the reporters were waiting for a response while DiBella, and I looked confused.

The reporter continued in Spanish until Lou cut him off, then pointed at me and said, "This guy speaks perfect English." The reporter botched my identity, but I knew I was a step closer to getting the recognition I deserved.

Those positive visions were what I needed
to keep me focused on the future instead
of my current circumstances.

———————————

LESSON

CHAPTER 21

Comeback Trail

I n 2016, I felt like I was on the verge of making it. I knew big money was on the way, but my spending habits acted like big money had already arrived. Aside from traveling expenses, I purchased the new red Camaro I wanted before my fight with Abel Ramos and splurged on a few other frivolous expenditures.

The timing of taking on more expenses couldn't have been any worse. Although my bank account was nearing E, I planned on refilling it after my next fight within the following weeks or months, but things don't always go as planned.

Sparring was a major reason for my rapid development. Many good fighters cherry-pick sparring partners so they can try new things and not be pushed to the limit. The Houston fighting scene gave me plenty of competition that pushed me to new heights. I had the opportunity to consistently spar with talented fighters in different weight classes and various styles.

On a casual sparring day, I took a punch that caused concern as soon as it landed. A sparring partner used to throw his uppercuts awkwardly with his thumb out, and one caught me in the eye. We heard a pop when the awkward uppercut landed. I immediately stepped out of the ring and started throwing up.

Dizziness and wooziness took over. Having that type of reaction to a punch is usually a sign of brain damage. Things became silent in the gym because the pain penetrated past my tolerance. It persisted the following day, and I had no choice but to see a doctor.

Twenty minutes into my visit, the doctor reentered the room. I saw his mouth moving, but didn't hear a word. When the doctor could tell my mind drifted elsewhere, he repeated himself and said, "Regis, you have a serious eye injury. Your orbital bone is popped. This is the bone behind your eye. If you push it, your eye will fall into your head. You'll never be able to box again."

Minutes later, I cried loud enough in my car to drown out the radio. Boxing wasn't all I knew, but it was all I wanted. I informed my corner about the severity of the injury, and they encouraged me to get a second opinion. Being the persistent person I am, I got a second, third, and fourth opinion. Even if they agreed with the first opinion, I knew God had the final say.

My career was in jeopardy during its infancy stages, but I knew it was just another obstacle to overcome. What the first doctor told me fell on deaf ears. I never stopped training, and I sought past his advice.

The second doctor suggested that I get a plate in my eye and have surgery. Stopping at his opinion wasn't an option. The third doctor suggested that I take one or two years off. I finally got the answer I was looking for from the fourth doctor.

When I received my fourth opinion several months after the injury occurred, the doctor informed me that my orbital healed stronger than before. God showed me how rewarding faith can be. I always believed that I could shake back from the career-threatening injury. I could have easily followed the first doctor's advice and ended everything there or let myself go mentally and physically until I was medically cleared. Instead, I grinded through the uncertainty and was ready to reenter the ring after gaining clearance.

The setback made me think about my legacy more than ever and tested my faith. If my career ended with no world titles, I would have felt the ultimate defeat. A ranking with nothing to show for it did nothing for me. A legacy-based perspective made me more intentional about my goals.

While my eye healed, my finances were depleted. I couldn't fight for several months, but the bills were still coming. I saw my financial situation caving in once I couldn't keep up with my car note.

Primo helped me save face. Well, at least to some degree. He took over my car note and keys for a short time.

Consequently, I started driving my wife's compact Chevy Spark.

No one could cover for me after the obvious downgrade. Every time someone questioned me about my car, I would lie with a straight face and prideful heart and say my friend was borrowing it. I didn't include the part that my friend was paying the note.

I developed one of my most beneficial routines during one of the toughest times in my life. It's one thing to struggle while you're young, but it's another thing to struggle as an adult. As a youth, we are new to the world and have not developed a sense of normalcy yet.

While leading a household consisting of a young baby, a new marriage, mold, and occasionally paid utility bills, I knew life had to improve. My wife would heat water on the stove to bathe during the winter. Necessities seemed like luxuries during a winter when our lights were turned off twice due to unpaid bills, and we couldn't get any hot water.

I'd be so tired from boxing most days that I didn't bother to heat the water. After realizing many athletes take ice baths, I began researching the benefits of cold showers. Once I realized the struggle was worth the benefits, I incorporated cold showers into my daily routine.

Months later, I had to turn to another place for help. Marc stopped us from being evicted four months in a row. During those months, mold began spreading in our one-bedroom apartment. I would routinely gaze into my wife and son's eyes and visualize us in a mansion. Those positive visions were what I needed to keep me focused on the future instead of my current circumstances.

An underrated element of a relationship is how a person gets along with their spouse's family. I was thankful to mesh perfectly with Raquel's family. Marc grew into a father figure and introduced me to a lifestyle I wanted for myself and my family.

Marcia and Marc's son, Jason, became a little brother of mine, and I had a sibling-like relationship with Raquel's sister, Rafa. The relationships formed effortlessly. I never had to put on a front for them or pretend to be someone other than myself. Many people wear masks for years and decades to get along with their significant other's families.

My fight at the end of the comeback trail was in Mississippi against Wilfredo Buelcas. I thought that would be my last fight under Tee, but he was adamant about me owing him another fight because of my injury.

I felt the same anger I experienced before my fight against Aaron Herrera when I didn't make weight. It had been a feeling I grew accustomed to, and I wanted freedom from it. The result against Buelcas was the same as Herrera. I ended both fights in less than a minute. A right hand to the body earned me a first-round knockout victory and an 8th place ranking by the WBC. I had knocked out 12 of my previous 13 opponents and was ready for another step-up fight.

You catch something new every time
you watch the same fight, just like you
notice something new every time
you read the same book.

———————

LESSON

CHAPTER 22

Who Did You Beat?

B eing one fight away from becoming a free agent was something to celebrate. I felt like I was close to becoming a star with the right management backing me. The 2017 NBA All-Star weekend in New Orleans gave me a taste of what living as a star would be like. More people knew who I was throughout the city, but I remained under the radar on the national scene.

At this stage, being around celebrities had a different meaning than during my childhood. I wanted to examine how they carried themselves outside of their craft and how they socialized and networked. While out, I connected with Floyd Mayweather Jr., one of the best people I could have interacted with at the time.

I instantly grasped the correlation between a champion's lifestyle inside and outside the ring. The massive bodyguards, flashy jewelry, foreign cars, designer clothing, and beautiful women surrounding him would have made a person who didn't know anything about boxing recognize that he was a star.

Mutual friends introduced us, and I didn't hesitate to tell him what I had done so far in the boxing world. At the time,

19-0 with 16 knockouts sounded like an impressive resume to me. For a moment, I thought he would be impressed with it, but he immediately asked, "Who did you beat?"

As I tried justifying my accomplishments, he respectfully repeated the same question. From that moment, a battery was in my back to put some successful names on my resume and knockout list. The timing of that interaction felt God-sent. He had been retired from boxing for two years and was months away from returning for his 50th victory.

After interacting with Mayweather, I thought deeper about what I wanted my career to stand for. He carved out his legacy and became the highest earner in boxing history. I was only 19 fights into my career, but many analysts tried boxing me in and branding me as just a power puncher. I am that, plus more, but I hadn't been pushed to the point of having to use many other skills in my repertoire.

My last fight under Tee was a test mentally and physically. I knew that it was our last fight together, but I had to carry on as if it was just another fight. It was anything but that. Raquel was pregnant with our second child, Khalessi. I was facing another step up in competition, and I had to face the inevitable and prolonged split.

The stakes were higher than ever. Some "experts" said my streak would end when I fought Joel Diaz, who was 23-0 at the time with 19 knockouts. In a sense, I was punching my way to financial freedom.

Joel Diaz and I had different routes to the same destination and mirroring amateur and professional careers. He had 95 amateur fights compared to my 94, and we were a combined 42-0 with high knockout percentages.

On the contrary, my opponent was bred to become a boxer. His father was a reputable boxing trainer. My fight with Diaz was an opportunity for a promotion in the boxing world from prospect to contender.

The dynamics at the top of the division shifted that April when Julius Indongo defeated Ricky Burns to become a unified champion by capturing two world titles. He held the WBA and IBF belts, and Terence Crawford held the WBC and WBO belts. Everyone in the division was on the outside looking in because Crawford and Indongo were on a collision course to see who would become the undisputed champion.

At this point, I had become a regular on ShoBox, and I was headlining another televised event. The circumstances surrounding my fight heightened the energy in New York. Diaz and I would be fighting during the International Boxing Hall-of-Fame induction weekend.

Our fight was billed as "two highly regarded undefeated prospects fighting for a chance to move on to Showtime Championship Boxing." ShoBox was a proving ground and platform for prospects to face their toughest tests while moving up the ranks. Our fight was the epitome of what the event was designed for.

Diaz and I traded blows that entertained the crowd during the first round, but only one of us was hurt. When I wind up my punches before throwing them, that usually means I realize my opponent is hurt and close to going down. At the end of the first round, I began winding up my punches and walking him down. Ten seconds into the second round, my senses proved to be true. I threw several right jabs to get my distance and set Diaz up for a left hand to the body that dropped him to the canvas.

My practice translated to the fight on the final knockdown. Bobby knew Diaz liked to throw wide punches, so we worked on short sweeping punches during training camp. A sweeping left hook swept my opponent off his feet for the fourth and final knockdown, forcing him to do his second somersault of the night.

Making a tough opponent look easy motivated me to call out bigger names in the division during the post-fight interview in the ring. I was a high-risk and low-reward for big names at the time, so I had to use my opportunity to call them out. I knew I graduated to a new level past ShoBox. Most importantly, I was finally in a position to capitalize financially on my talents.

Although other management companies were lined up to offer me lucrative deals, I still took a meeting with Tee. I knew things wouldn't go past that first contract, but the second contract proposal felt like a slap in the face and officially ended our partnership. Regardless of our business dealings, Tee and I established a bond that will last a lifetime.

He played an intricate part during the early stages of my career and was one of the first people to believe in me. I am forever thankful for his contributions to my career and our memories together. I will always wish him the best.

...

My next fight would be the first one without management and Tee in my corner. I had ideas of who I wanted to sign with, but taking care of my next opponent was the priority at hand. The four world titles were up for grabs when Terence Crawford moved up to the 147-pound division after defeating Julius Indongo.

Maurice Hooker was scheduled to fight Terry Flanagan for the WBO belt, Kiryl Relikh was scheduled to fight Rances Barthelemy for the WBA title, and Mikey Garcia and Sergey Lipinets were scheduled to fight for the IBF title.

It was a four-person race for the WBC belt. I was ranked #2 in the division, but the winner of #1 vs. #3 would be fighting for the world title. My fight against Viktor Postol was for the

Interim WBC title and to become the mandatory challenger of the victor between Jose Ramirez and Amir Imam.

Postol and I were scheduled to fight in Miami, Florida, on March 9, 2018. In February, he fractured his thumb and dropped out of the fight. The fight date remained the same, but the location and opponent changed. I would be fighting Julius Indongo at Deadwood Mountain Grand, a casino and resort in South Dakota, on Showtime.

The boxing world would have no choice but to mention my name at the top and for world title fights if I was successful against a former unified world champion and Olympian. Julius Indongo was the most accomplished fighter I faced at that point in my pro career. A unified champion has a different pedigree from top contenders and prospects.

The fight was in Deadwood, South Dakota, but it felt like I was training for a fight in Las Vegas. I knew our fight would draw more coverage than all my previous ones. This was a prime opportunity to showcase my talents on the big stage.

Watching film on my opponent isn't a major part of my fight preparation. After dissecting a few minutes of their previous fights, I am already convinced they can't beat me. Bobby watches film on my upcoming opponents to help me prepare, but I prefer to watch boxers that inspire me. The Mike Tyson vs. Leon Spinks fight in 1990 for undisputed heavyweight champion of the world was one of the fights I studied to prepare for Julius Indongo.

I knew Tyson made quick work of Spinks, but you catch something new every time you watch the same fight, just like you notice something new every time you read the same book. What was meant for me to catch happened before the fight started.

When the cameras panned in on Mike Tyson in the dressing room, he was violently punching the wall. His punches on the wall looked as if they had the power to put holes in a mountain. His opponent was on the other side of the wall. I can only imagine how that made Spinks feel before the fight, and I wanted to give Indongo that same feeling.

When my team and I got settled in the dressing room that night in Deadwood, South Dakota, I had two things on my mind - put my hands on Indongo and stop him before Crawford did. A third thing entered my mind when I spotted the dressing room wall and heard Indongo and his team on the other side. A few people in his corner tried to get in my head at the press conference, but I had something for them and their fighter. After my hands were taped, I planted my feet a few inches away from the wall and began letting off combinations on it.

I couldn't hear past the punches, but I knew the chatter died down on the other side of the wall. Once the wall began dismantling and I got my message across, Bobby calmed me down until it was time to unleash that energy in the ring.

As soon as the bell rang, I slipped into my rhythm. I knew he would come out aggressive, but he was unsure how I would come out. After slipping a two-punch combination, I landed a right jab that knocked him off his pivot. His punch combinations became repetitive until he threw three in a row toward the end of the round.

Once the ten-second notifier sounded, I landed a hook to the stomach that took his wind. It was the same punch that Crawford used to knock him out in the third round. When he grimaced, I followed with a left hand that knocked him off his feet. My opponent looked like he didn't know what hit him as the referee rattled off a 9-count. He was saved by the bell momentarily.

Once the 2nd round started, I began walking him down and looking for my opening. After he threw a lazy right hand, I countered with a sweeping left hook that sent him into the ropes. When I saw the opportunity to stop my opponent one round before Crawford did, I finished my mission. I knocked him down three times in the second round and ended the fight with a violent left hand.

Typically, after a victory, I would run toward my supporters and express the rush I felt from winning. I did that, plus more once I knocked my opponent down for the third time in thirty seconds and showed the world I was on a new level.

After my routine celebration, I saw a camera approaching me in my peripheral. Once it panned in on me, I stuck my chest out and yelled, "That's a statement right there! At 140 pounds, I'm the best at this shit! Ain't nobody fucking with me! I'm the best at this shit! Second round! Crawford did it in the third round, and I did it in two! That's easy work!"

People will mainly remember you for your
failures or shortcomings instead of the wins
it took for you to get there.

———————

LESSON

CHAPTER 23

New Orleans Boxing

There is no such thing as a sure thing in boxing. Jose Ramirez was scheduled as my mandatory fight since he beat Amir Imam for the WBC Super Lightweight Title. I went to their fight in Madison Square Garden and began seeing the plot unfold. Top Rank promoted Jose Ramirez. Bob Arum, Top Rank Founder and CEO, said he would like to pair Ramirez and me in separate fights on the same card before we meet in the ring.

Instead of allowing Ramirez to face me next for the world title, Top Rank offered me a step-aside fight deal and promoted my next fight against Juan Jose Velasco. I would face a high-level opponent, earn a lucrative payday, and be able to choose the location. However, I wouldn't get the opportunity to become a world champion.

Boxing may be the last sport you want to waste time in. Aside from successful names on my resume, I needed accolades to accompany them. The location and what I would be fighting for made the next fight one of my most meaningful.

Sharing a universal pain and love with everyone from New Orleans makes me want to bring the city healing and inspiration. I already started the healing aspect during the early part of my career by participating in charity events, speaking at schools, and donating. On July 14, 2018, I would get a chance to inspire the city by fighting at the New Orleans Lakefront Arena for an opportunity to enter the World Boxing Super Series tournament. Eight of the top fighters in my division would enter a tournament where the winner would take home several million dollars, world titles, and the Muhammad Ali Trophy.

The promotional campaign for my first big fight back home provided me an opportunity to show more of my personality to the media and public. I quickly saw why Top Rank is a top-notch and legendary promotional company. They collaborated with Lou DiBella to put together a great night of boxing for my city.

While preparing for the fight, I met two of the newest and biggest personalities in the boxing world. During the media workout, Teofimo Lopez's father began shouting, "My son is the best boxer in here! He is the biggest star here! He'll beat anybody in this building and world!" After his rant, he approached me and said, "You and my son need to fight each other. You two would make each other very rich."

I grinned and responded, "I'm already rich."

Teo, an Olympian for Honduras in 2016, was 9-0 at the time and co-headlining the card. His father was onto something and spoke life into his son's career. Teofimo would eventually become a highly accomplished world champion and a desirable opponent for me.

The energy he put into his son showed how impactful speaking life into someone can be. I had it on my mind to speak life into the youth back home. While interacting with the 200+ kids I purchased tickets for, I wondered what it would have been like to have that opportunity as a child. Their presence, along with the people I grew up with, people who watched me grow up, and others from my hometown, made me want to give my best performance ever. That gave me a different level of pressure I hadn't experienced before.

Bringing major boxing back to New Orleans was deeper than my fight. Several New Orleans boxers were on the undercard, the city was given a positive event to be excited about, and the city profited from the event. Boxers, media, and fans were coming from across the world to watch a professional boxing event I headlined and helped make happen. This fight was a testament to how far I made it and my love for New Orleans.

Fighting back home on the big stage made me think about the legendary boxers from my state who came before me. The top-rated boxers in Louisiana history, such as Tony Canzoneri, Joe Brown, Willie Pastrono, Ralph Dupas, and Pete Herman, were all world-class boxers, but their styles differed from mine. Respectively, their knockout percentages were Brown 30%,

Canzoneri 25%, Pastrano 17%, Dupas 14%, and Herman 13%. My knockout percentage at the time was 81%.

Harry Wills, a historic Louisiana fighter with knockout power, made me more thankful for the opportunity. Willis was born 100 years before me and knocked out half of his opponents. Boxing historians view Wills as one of the biggest victims of racism in boxing. Sometimes, we have to analyze our predecessor's struggles to understand our challenges better.

I felt that I should have been a world champion by then, but my obstacles to becoming a world champion didn't compare to the ones Harry Wills faced. He was ranked as the number one challenger for the throne, but was denied the opportunity for a title fight. Becoming the Heavyweight Champion of the World is one of the most prominent accolades in society. No black fighters were allowed that opportunity between the reigns of Jack Johnson (1908) and Joe Louis (1937). Johnson's victory led to a deadly riot, and Wills felt the aftereffects of it. Wills was positioned to challenge Jack Dempsey for the title in 1926. They signed a contract to fight in 1925, but Dempsey stated that he would no longer fight Black boxers after winning the title. That didn't stop Wills from having a legendary career. He held the World Colored Heavyweight Championship three times and was inducted into the International Boxing Hall-of-Fame in 1992, 34 years after his death.

New Orleans boxing history dates back to 1832, and I was about to become a major part of it. Regardless of how far back boxing dates in New Orleans, the city is an afterthought regarding boxing epicenters in the United States, such as Las Vegas, California, Philadelphia, and New York.

The New Orleans boxing scene experienced a four-year stretch from 1978 to 1982 when Muhammad Ali won his last professional bout in the Superdome, and other legendary fighters such as Roberto Duran and Sugar Ray Leonard squared off. A Roy Jones Jr. title defense in 2000 initiated an 18-year stretch of no major boxing events for the city where football historically dominated the sports scene and news headlines.

Ending the 18-year stretch created a new level of pressure I never experienced. Early into my professional career, I realized how bringing major boxing back to New Orleans could positively impact the city. Aside from generating revenue, boxing could serve as a positive outlet in a city where violence, poverty, and miseducation are entrenched in the culture. Many people forgot or were unaware of the ties New Orleans has with boxing. My event was a reminder that New Orleans is a great city to host major boxing events.

Until that point in my career, I had the mindset to let my work inside the ring speak for itself. My record spoke volumes, but my voice needed to be heard before my first big fight in my city. I fought in Metairie, Louisiana, for my 5th fight and Gretna,

Louisiana, for my 6th fight, but those bouts were nowhere close to this magnitude.

My fight in Metairie was at a hotel, and the one in Gretna was at a Heritage Festival. Neither was mentioned in the local papers or led to significant steps in my career. Although this fight would be shown on ESPN and covered by plenty of media outlets, I worked harder than ever outside the ring by promoting the fight.

Regardless of how far I made it in life, I remember the feeling of being a kid searching for direction and a way out. Impacting the school system, community, and playgrounds that raised me was a priority of mine once I became successful. I spent several weeks leading up to the fight, speaking at public schools, promoting the fight relentlessly, visiting boxing gyms, and interviewing with radio stations and media outlets. Typically, it didn't matter if I fought in front of five or 500 people, but I wanted to pack the building for this one.

I slept at my grandparents' house before my fights in Metairie and Gretna and drove to them. For this fight, my team and I were booked to stay in a 5-star hotel downtown and escorted to the fight in a limousine. Focusing on how much further I had to go instead of how far I made it kept me hungry and discontent.

As favorable as fighting in your hometown may seem, there are unseen pitfalls. Failing on your hometown stage is the worst place on earth to fail. People will mainly remember you for your failures or shortcomings instead of the wins it took for you to get there.

Many boxers who were deemed as the favorite for a fight in their hometown lost in a fashion that stuck with them beyond that fight. Pressure busts pipes and dreams. The levels of pressure picked up each day leading up to the fight, along with the pitfalls of fighting in your hometown.

The distractions started as soon as I exited the limo when I arrived at the arena. A friend of a friend was waiting for me by the entrance. He quickly approached me and asked if he could pretend to be my bodyguard. His strategy worked because the cameras bombarded me after him, and I complied to regain focus on the task at hand.

The friend of a friend's presence wasn't bothersome aside from the unexpectedness. Having a "bodyguard" aligned with the new experience of fighting on a bigger stage. The bothersome part happened when the crowd began piling up in the locker room.

I expected my close friends and a few other members of my entourage to be there, but they were only a small fraction of the crowd. Strangers began appearing, and people around me were playing while I was preparing for war. Altering my routine before the fight made me uncomfortable in the place where I'm most comfortable. Intentionally making myself uncomfortable on a consistent basis paid off when I needed it the most.

My nerves usually settle once I make it to the locker room before a fight. I know I am only moments away from a time that's been replaying non-stop in my mind for months. The environment in the locker room bottled up my nerves and intensified them. Consequently, I had to take them with me to the ring.

Regardless of which slum or project you are from in the US, you have the opportunity to live out your dream and become financially independent. Those same opportunities don't exist in many countries outside of the US.

———

LESSON

CHAPTER 24

Fighting In Your Hometown

My surroundings were darker than closed eyes as I stood behind the curtain preparing for my ring walk. Built-up butterflies swarmed once highlights of my favorite boxers broke the darkness and appeared on the jumbotron, illuminating the New Orleans Lakefront Arena. Throughout my life, I viewed boxing highlights and fights more than my reflection. Regardless of the repetitiveness, I get lost in each moment and enter a new world where nothing else exists.

Thunderous roars from my hometown crowd reeled me back to reality. After the Mardi Gras Indians started chanting and everyone in the arena gave me their undivided attention, I took the longest walk ever to the ring. My 21st fight was a reintroduction to my hometown crowd. Most of the audience knew me as Regis Prograis, but now I was known in the boxing world as Regis Rougarou Prograis.

The custom-fitted mask exemplifying my boxing alter-ego defeated half of its purpose that night. Aside from showmanship, it's worn to block distractions on the ring walk.

A different distraction appeared with every step I took toward the ring.

The ring walk is an opportunity for a boxer to share his vibe with the arena and viewers. This is when the sideshow becomes the main show. I was caught up in the show on the way to the ring, where my opponent awaited me as I led the Mardi Gras Indians and got accompanied by my team and entourage.

My mind was led astray by distractions and anxious energy until a right hand awakened me during the middle of the first round. The punch didn't hurt or cause a reaction from the crowd, but it made me lock back in on the mission at hand.

After overcoming Hurricane Katrina, packing the arena, and surviving a wild upbringing in one of the most dangerous cities in the world, losing in front of my hometown crowd wasn't an option. Moments after getting hit, I returned a right hand that felt like a car wreck to the ribs and set the tone for the fight.

My previous five bouts lasted a total of ten rounds because I found my rhythm quickly. Rhythm is the key to finding your zone, whether dancing, boxing, writing, sex, or conversation. Regardless of its importance, it took me longer than usual to find it.

Knocking out my opponent is always the goal, but I never intend to damage my opponent past our fight. Unfortunately, that's often what happens. It was a competitive first round, but after the opening round, I began damaging my opponent.

I chipped away at the knockout and broke him down piece by piece. Although most of my power punches to the head landed with concussive force, body shots did the most damage to him. By the third round, he began fighting with one of the lowest guards I ever saw to protect his body. My adversary was overly concerned about my overhand left that dropped my last several opponents. That left his body open throughout the entire fight.

I felt him getting closer to the canvas during the third and fourth rounds. He was fighting in survival mode. I finally found my opening to drop him during the fourth round when I landed a punch on his solar plex that made him grimace and fall to his knees.

I thought the fight would be over within a few seconds, but Velasco rose to his feet and used them for the rest of the round. It's evident in a fighter's eyes and body language when their heart is taken, and they don't want to fight anymore. As brutal as it may sound, I enjoy delivering pain to an opponent, but the fun diminishes when my opponent is defenseless, and he remains in the ring after his will is gone.

My opponent's corner failed him in a few ways. Their initial game plan was to survive until the 6th round, then try to take control of the fight. It's hard to thrive when you are just trying to survive. Playing it safe and misinformed placed them at a disadvantage before the fight started. There was no chance of me getting tired by the 6th round.

The other corner put their fighter in an even worse position after the 5th round when a left hook to the body put him back on the canvas. When Velasco returned to the corner, he told his trainer he couldn't go anymore. His trainer convinced him to come back out. Regardless of how much a trainer prepares their fighter, the fighter is the only one absorbing the pain and punishment. After the 6th round, Velasco's trainer said, "Don't do this to me! Don't quit on me now! Just go out there and try to survive."

The next two knockdowns happened after I barely touched my opponent, but his trainer made him keep going when everyone else in the arena could see he had nothing left. The only weapon he had left in his arsenal was his heart, and that signifies a fighter's gas light is under E and about to run out. Neither one of us could believe we were still in the ring. Once the fight was waved off, it looked like I had just clocked out from another day at the office, but it was anything but another typical workday.

The meaning of each fight extends far beyond the win column. Joy isn't inclusive with every victory, and it takes an in-depth level of understanding to comprehend that. After my past several victories, I stormed around the ring, called out other fighters, and proudly yelled how I felt about myself as a boxer. I felt relieved after delivering an 8th round knockout in front of my home crowd, but my instincts didn't let me celebrate as usual. As the crowd cheered my name, I knew that wasn't my best performance. My notoriety grew after the victory, but the world had much more to learn about Regis Prograis.

Before the fight, I had a premonition that it would be a victorious night but not a joyous one. Most of my visions come to fruition, but not exactly how I visualize them. I imagined this victory bringing me the ultimate sunshine. Instead, a dark cloud hovered over my head as soon as I exited the ring.

The background of my post-fight interviews sounded like they were hosted at a nightclub. Before and after the fight, I was surrounded by my team and friends, cousins of acquaintances, and people who only wanted to be on the scene. Having people playing around me while I was preparing and decompressing from war threw off my energy before and after the fight.

The friend of a friend came in handy to settle the noise around me before the fight, but he was nowhere to be found when I needed him again after it. Two of my friends were a few verbal jabs away from being the last fight of the night. Post-fight in the locker room was usually when my team and I exhaled and reflected on the hard work it took to make the victory possible. Now, the attention was elsewhere.

Once things were diffused, Tony, my friend and business partner, rushed to tell me that my mother needed me. She was on the verge of fainting when I spotted her surrounded by a crowd in the hallway. She called for me while I was within arm's reach, then passed out.

Everything around me moved a million miles a minute, but my world paused while my mom was rushed to the hospital. My mother's health was restored, but the magical feeling of a night I fantasized about for more than a decade couldn't be.

The day after the fight signified what type of trip it was. Looking out for someone else's kid enticed them to look out for me and one of my kids. Khalessi is a reflection of my mother and me. Ever since Khalessi could walk, she led our family when we walked places, even if she didn't know where she was going. She's athletic and adventurous like me, and bossy like my mother. It's their way or the highway. Khalessi chose the highway for Raquel and me when she decided to color on the hotel walls as if she was a mural artist. I was looking at a pricey hotel bill until the maintenance man recognized me from speaking at his son's school earlier that week. Impacting others while not looking for anything in return earned me an unexpected blessing.

. . .

I brought major boxing back to New Orleans and positioned myself to become the first world champion from my city since 1963. Taking the biggest step of my career in front of my city felt like a storybook moment, aside from what went on behind the scenes. We were walking into the spotlight together. I made it through the hard road and had my city on my back in the boxing world.

My next stop in the boxing world was in Europe. *Who would have thought that learning how to fight on the streets of New Orleans would have led me across the world*, was what I thought as I walked around Moscow, Russia. I was flown to Russia for the announcement of the World Boxing Super Series tournament. I had no choice but to size up the other competitors while there. They did the same to me because I was predicted as the favorite to win the tournament. I only sized up two people in Russia - Josh Taylor and Ivan Baranchyk.

Traveling to three different continents in one month felt out of this world. Until then, I lived a frugal lifestyle. I knew what it was like to make a lot of money and lose it, but now I was at the point where I could enjoy the fruits of my labor with peace of mind.

After the tournament was announced, I knew I would be in for another long grind. I had already been through a lengthy one making it down the hard road, so I wanted to get away and enjoy myself before locking in for the tournament. During the post-fight interview in New Orleans, I shouted out my wife's hometown in Brazil. I knew they were watching and awaiting our arrival. We planned on visiting for 30 days.

When I returned to Brazil, I didn't feel like I was visiting a foreign land. Although I wasn't fluent in Portuguese yet, my in-laws and other Brazilians embraced me as if I were part of their culture. One thing I love about Brazilian culture is how little material possessions mean to them.

Most of the people I met only had a few items of clothing and one pair of shoes and didn't even have enough money to say that they were living check-to-check. Nonetheless, their smiles and happiness would lead you to believe they had everything. In reality, they did have it all. They had an understanding of life's most important aspects. Hurricane Katrina helped me comprehend the same concepts.

The root of many Americans' unhappiness stems from what they don't have. Expensive clothing is an intricate part of inner-city culture. If kids didn't have name-brand clothes when I was growing up, they were the main people getting made fun of. People in Brazil didn't care about what you had or didn't have. That is part of what makes their culture so unique and organic.

One of the biggest things that reminded me of New Orleans was their party lifestyle. On this trip to Brazil, I experienced the favelas for the first time. I thought I knew what a wild party was until I partied there. They hosted a block party like no other. Mardi Gras and Bourbon Street in New Orleans are the only things I can compare it to, except they had these parties every weekend.

My wife's neighborhood is so popular that Jay-Z rapped about it on his Blueprint 3 album track "Real As It Gets" when he said, "Hov's the audio equivalent to braille. That's why they feel me in the favelas in Brazil and Waterhouse because real recognize real."

The party in the favelas was policed by people who lived there. They sported AK-47s wrapped around their necks to keep things in check. If they caught you recording or taking pictures of anything, you would be lucky for them to tell you to put your phone away. I watched them destroy three phones within my first thirty minutes there. I didn't realize how much phones took away from a party until I partied in Brazil.

People were freely being themselves without fear of judgment. There were all types of gangster things occurring, but ironically, these things kept the peace. Although there wasn't a police presence at the event, they were surrounding the event. The favelas are on a hill. People wouldn't leave the party until after sunrise the next day, and the police would be waiting in position to pull partygoers over.

Thirty seconds after we left the party, I was pulled over. I rented a Duster when I arrived in Brazil, which is a basic jeep. However, most people there didn't have cars, so they viewed the basic jeep as a luxury vehicle. The cops were suspicious of us.

Raquel and her friends riding with us communicated to the officers. They showed them my championship belts and told them I was American. Then they eased up. Americans are treated as royalty over there. Their perception is that every American has money and is from places depicted in movies like Las Vegas, Los Angeles, and New York. The cops let us go, but we were pulled over again a few minutes later. Regardless of the hassle, it didn't damper the experience.

A common sentiment about New Orleans people is that they want to marry someone from New Orleans because of our unique culture. Many outsiders of the New Orleans culture don't understand or can't get with it, regardless of how much they like it. My wife acts like a New Orleanian and seamlessly fits in amongst my friends, family, and city. Her culture is a reflection of my city thousands of miles away. I was reminded of the similarities and differences during this visit to Brazil.

On this trip, we celebrated Khalessi's second birthday. Renato, Raquel's childhood friend, became my friend, also. His child and Khalessi have the same birthday. I rented a hall, hired some entertainment, and threw a memorable joint party for the kids connected at birth, like Cedric and me.

In New Orleans and Brazil, kid parties turn into adult parties. I didn't think twice about footing the bill for the event, but I thought long and hard about Renato's gratitude for me financing it. Most men are molded to conceal their emotions, but my new friend in Brazil was in tears because of how appreciative he was. Renato vented about how he would never be able to do such a thing by himself for his kids. The lack of upward mobility in his country put things in perspective and made me thankful to be from the United States. Regardless of which slum or project you are from in the US, you have the opportunity to live out your dream and become financially independent. Those same opportunities don't exist in many countries outside of the US.

Bad luck is often confused with making
the same mistakes repeatedly.

———————

LESSON

CHAPTER 25

World Boxing Super Series

B ig-time boxing was back to stay in New Orleans. For the first fight of the tournament, I was able to pick my opponent and location. I chose my city and the toughest opposition available, Terry Flanagan. Flanagan was 33-1, a former world champion, fought five title defenses, and hadn't been dropped in his entire career.

Bad luck is often confused with making the same mistakes repeatedly. I knew my mistakes in my previous fight wouldn't be repeated. Focusing more on boxing than promoting the fight deepened my focus. An event leading up to the fight loosened things up in my corner.

Evins is always the tensest person on my team leading up to the fight. You would think he was getting in the ring based on his demeanor and militant ways during training camp. One thing he and I have in common is a chip on our shoulder. His background is in track and training, which was his entry into the boxing world. He's grown to make strength and conditioning for boxing his specialty and is passionate about proving it. His passionate rants are a continuous form of entertainment for us.

Bobby gave us something else to laugh at with Evins. He told Evins that Terry Flanagan's strength and conditioning coach was telling people that my strength and conditioning coach doesn't know what he is doing. Evins began pacing around like he was about to exit the locker room for the ring walk.

When we crossed paths with Terry Flanagan's team, Evins approached them, then went off. We had his back, but he was ready to go 1 on 7 with them. They all looked confused while we tried to hide our laughs.

Bobby laughed the hardest, but I didn't know why until later when I found out he made the whole thing up. Times like those are priceless and can't be created by people you don't naturally vibe with. Leading up to fights is preparation for war, but there needs to be a balance to the militance.

My love for boxing was on full display for 12 rounds. That night, I got as many oohs and ahs for defense as my offense. I got stronger as the fight progressed and dominated the first several rounds.

He tried stepping it up in the 7th round, but stepped into an even deeper hole in the 8th round when a hook dropped him to the canvas for the first time in his career. He was one of the rare opponents who recovered after I knocked him down. My motivation to show that I could box at a high level and that I wasn't just a power puncher may have prolonged the fight.

His best round was the 11th, but I connected with several hard shots during the final round and left no mystery about who would be announced the winner. His ability to withstand those shots in the late stages of the fight and last the distance earned my respect.

It felt like I could have gone several more rounds once the fight ended. Sometimes, it's not about what we do, and it's about how we do it. Not many boxers can go twelve rounds, and even fewer have anything left in the tank after that. I answered all my critics' questions without saying a word by going 12 rounds, barely getting touched, and dominating a former world champion.

Defeating a world champion positioned me to become one. My deal with Top Rank for the step-aside fight made me further evaluate the value of money and belts for fights. The payday was great, but an opportunity to become a world champion by fighting Jose Ramirez would have been greater.

My next opponent, Kiryl Relikh, was the last person standing in my way of becoming a world champion. Aside from getting a chance to perform in my home state, his WBA Super Lightweight title was on the line. I was confident about fighting Relikh before Bobby began preparing me for him. Our relationship started with a unique connection, and he became family to me.

Bobby and I were only training together for a few months when he made time out of his schedule to be at the hospital for my son's birth. He attended my family events, and we had never-ending conversations. Helping him achieve his goals was important to me. I had the opportunity to become a world champion on his birthday. There was no way I could let him down on the day he was born.

The circumstances at hand made me reflect on my legacy. This was a step toward immortality and accomplishing something that would live on forever. Louisiana didn't have a face of boxing, and I became it. Learning about other historic New Orleans boxers made me want to create a wave of Louisiana boxers after me. I don't want there to be another 50+ year streak for the next world champion to come from New Orleans.

As bad as I wanted to bring my third fight in a row back to New Orleans, it didn't end up being an option like I thought it would be. The next best location was a destination between my first and second home. Lafayette, Louisiana, is near the halfway point between New Orleans and Houston.

The mission of bringing big-time boxing back to New Orleans was already accomplished. Now, I wanted to bring it to another part of my home state. Walking to the ring with my son gave me an extra level of motivation to advance to the finals of the tournament and become a world champion.

My opponent came to the ring with the wrong game plan. He began trying to walk me down at the beginning of the fight. Throwing power punches and missing wears on fighters' confidence and energy. I made him pay for his mistakes by making him feel my power in the first round.

Once my opponent threw a right hand and overextended, I cocked back and punched him in the liver hard enough to leave prints on it. He immediately ran away in the other direction after he felt the pain of standing in my way to becoming a world champion.

An opponent that had never been stopped was already on a knee toward the end of the first round. The referee counted to seven before he rose to his feet. After the knockdown, it looked like we were playing a game of tag to close the round.

In the second round, I began teeing off on him. I set a repetitive narrative for the fight when I landed a powerful shot to the body, then bobbed and weaved under Relikh's counterpunches.

After the second round ended, my opponent hit me with a flush shot. The crowd was fully engaged. Their cheers turned into anger when my adversary connected. I was so locked in that I didn't take it personally and allow it to pull me out of my zone.

His punch didn't go unfelt and gave him a head start in the third round. A head start doesn't mean much against a determined person. Many others got a head start in boxing and life before me, but that never stopped me from overcoming the obstacle at hand.

After ducking under another three-punch combination and countering him with power, my opponent began losing hope. I felt him getting closer to the canvas after I snapped his head back with a left during the 5th round. My adversary's frustration showed through the blood and bruises on his face.

Showing pain isn't the only way I can feel a fighter is near their stopping point. When my opponent is visibly frustrated is another signifier. Relikh shook his head in disgust shortly after I snapped it back.

Relikh's trainer showed love and concern for him after the fifth round. Before the 6th round began, his trainer told him, "I care too much about you to let you go on like this." Halfway into the sixth, my opponent began looking like a punching bag.

The punching bag unraveled when I crouched down and exploded up with a left hook like Joe Frazier. That punch caused blood to fly out of the ring and his corner to stop the fight. Leaving Lafayette as the first world champion from Louisiana in more than a half-century propelled me into the history books and a showdown with the winner of Ivan Baranchyk and Josh Taylor.

A champion must act like one
during victory and defeat.

———————

LESSON

CHAPTER 26

Foreign Territory

An aspect of the tournament that differed from the rest of my career was that I had an idea of who I would fight next. Fighting Baranchyk and Taylor had been in the back of my mind since the beginning of the tournament. Their fight was in Scotland, Europe, two weeks after my semi-final bout.

Love for the sport of boxing unifies people from different backgrounds, races, and locations. Seeing how entrenched Europeans are in boxing deepened my love for their culture. Boxing schools for children are abundant, and most fans are knowledgeable and passionate. Regardless of my affinity for their culture, I envisioned the championship fight being on my turf.

I went to Scotland to watch Ivan Baranchyk vs. Josh Taylor and scout my next opponent. Their fight made me feel like a boxing fan as I became immersed in Josh Taylor's hometown crowd. I watched Ivan for years and heard about Josh for years.

Both were undefeated favorites to face me in the championship. Ivan and I fought on the same cards multiple times, and I knew more about his personality, strengths, and weaknesses. He had vicious knockout power, but was soft-spoken and didn't talk as much noise as the typical boxer.

I learned that Josh was the opposite as the tournament progressed. He still had the energy to talk shit to me after his unanimous decision against Ivan. His crowd roared him to victory, then booed me after the post-fight interview in the ring.

I shouldn't have expected cheers from his home crowd, but I wasn't expecting the boos filled with anger and fueled with alcohol. Traveling several thousand miles to attend the fight was a sign of respect. I embraced the negative reaction I never experienced with open arms. As they booed, I gestured that Taylor and I could fight in their home country to appease them, but they booed even louder.

The boos were the only blemish on my trip until it was time to leave. Experiencing another country due to boxing put me on a natural high the entire time. Having Primo and Tony with me heightened the experience even more. Our short time there wasn't enough, but I knew I was there for business.

My friends and I felt like outcasts in every aspect as we moved through a foreign land. We dressed, talked, and looked different from everyone we saw. Perhaps that was what led us to be detained at the airport for a few hours. It's easy to assume they singled us out because of our skin color, but I wondered if they would have treated us the same if we were dressed differently. I'm proud of my ethnicity and would never hide who I am, but that circumstance made me re-evaluate how I carried myself.

Life was elevating to new heights, and I knew it was my responsibility to look the part. Looking the part extended past what I wore every day. After experiencing a career-changing victory, I wanted to make a lifestyle change.

I was becoming a boxing star in the ring, but I wanted my stardom to extend beyond the boxing world. My new management team gave me an opportunity to do that. After parting ways with Tee, I signed with Churchill Management, which is owned by Hollywood stars and boxing enthusiasts Peter Berg and Mark Wahlberg.

California has always been a dream destination for me since I was a child, and that's where Churchill is based. Hollywood is the home of dreams worldwide, and I was in the midst of living through one. The vision of not leaving California after my 13th fight evolved and became reality.

Running into Leonard Ellerbe, CEO of Mayweather Promotions in LA, while being interviewed reminded me how far I had come. It reminded me of the conversation Floyd, and I had during the NBA All-Star break in New Orleans. Now, I could speak on champions I beat, and he acknowledged my accomplishments without me having to speak about them. My credentials became self-explanatory.

Regardless of my ascension financially and professionally, I was still frugal and hadn't fully begun enjoying the fruits of my labor yet. The suppression of my enjoyment and the opportunity to take my career to new heights led me to think about a new lifestyle. Sacrificing immediate gratification finally paid off.

When I returned from Scotland, I decided it was time for new surroundings. Shortly after becoming a world champion, I moved my family and I into a multi-million-dollar home in the suburbs of Los Angeles.

Regardless of how much I desired to be in LA, it was a challenging adjustment. My family and friends' presence gave me a little taste of home and temporarily tamed my quickly developed homesickness. Discomfort is a part of adjusting to new levels. As much as I hated the traffic and being away from home, I loved the beaches, opportunities, and other million things there are to love about Los Angeles.

While adapting to California, I was still adjusting to the business side of boxing. As cut and dry as a tournament may sound, circumstances weren't always that simple during the World Boxing Super Series. Fights were in jeopardy for other boxers and me. The tournament was behind schedule for several months, and boxers were prohibited from fighting outside the tournament.

My fight against Taylor was prolonged due to business and logistics matters. I was the #1 seed in the tournament, but they boxed me in about having to fight Josh Taylor in Europe. The concept was illogical to put the champion at a disadvantage and make him a visitor during a championship bout. The campaign for a neutral site fell on deaf ears.

While talks about fighting Taylor stalled during the summer of 2019, I kept myself busy outside the ring. I landed my first speaking role in a movie titled *Spenser Confidential*, traveled, and went spearfishing, deep sea diving, and skydiving.

Shortly after moving to California, several social media followers accused me of being scared to fight Josh Taylor in Europe. The baseless trolling and stalled negotiations led me to agree to fight Josh Taylor a few hundred miles away from his hometown and a few thousand miles away from mine.

Our fight for the Muhammad Ali trophy and three world titles was scheduled for October 26, 2019. All my training camps were similar, aside from the one for my first fight on TV and my first one outside the country. For this fight, we planned a three-part training camp. My training camp would be split between Houston, Los Angeles, and the United Kingdom. Putting in work with my team in Houston made me realize what I was missing. We were separated for the longest time in my career.

The culture of my training camps provides me with a much-needed balance. One of my favorite memories helped me feel at home on the other side of the country. Primo is a serial hustler, jack-of-all-trades, and avid dreamer. His hustles and talents ranged from breeding horses, racing RC cars, investing, art, rapping, selling dogs, cooking, and driving 18-wheelers. He was talented at every endeavor. In 2018, Primo had Forex on his mind and laid out an elaborate plot of how he was about to get rich and have a Lamborghini in six months.

Once Bobby objected to his plan, they got into a spirited and comical debate. Debating might be the thing we do the second most after training. The moment of watching them debate was much deeper than the laughs. I was thankful to grow with both of them from two different stages in my life.

Fighting in another country was a foreign experience for my team and me, so we didn't have any protocols set. Leaving for London three weeks before the fight initially sounded like a good plan. I wanted to adjust to their food, weather, and environment before the biggest fight of my life.

I received confirmation that I arrived at a new level shortly after I landed in London. Within several minutes of walking around the airport, multiple people recognized me. From that moment, I redefined my missions in Europe.

My initial goals were to win the belts and trophies, expose my family and friends to a new country, and represent my city in a foreign country. Making an impact in Europe and acquiring new fans were added to that list. The excitement in the fans' eyes I met at the airport made me want to spread that same joy to other boxing fans across the world.

The work I put into promoting the fight in London surpassed the excessive press run I did leading up to my first major fight in New Orleans. Being out and about in New Orleans and London are two different things.

I deeply appreciated the new environment, but it quickly lowered my morale. I only saw the sun once during my first week, and I missed my son's birthday. Most of my time was spent in isolation or promoting the event. My father told me to relax and remain focused, but I needed that time outside the Airbnb to lift my spirits. When I arrived in Europe, I was fired up to fight, but the fire could only burn for so long.

The gloom intensified in London on my fourth day there. Back in the States, another title shot occurred in Chicago on October 12, 2019. The fight for the IBF-USBA Super Welterweight title between Charles Conwell and Patrick Day went under many radars until the fight concluded. Spectators watching the undercard of Oleksandr Usyk's heavyweight debut witnessed a brutal knockout when Conwell knocked Day out. He remained motionless on the canvas and left the ring on a stretcher.

Day never regained consciousness and died on October 16. He was buried a few days before my fight with Taylor. His tragic fate, which all boxers potentially face when we step in the ring, was planted in my subconscious.

Gloom not only filled the skies of London and the boxing world. It also infiltrated my mental state and my opponent's world. Leading up to the fight, Josh lost his father-in-law, his trainer's sister passed away, and a stablemate lost a big fight.

Being a historian of the sport, I knew the obstacles I was up against. Almost every boxer I communicated with leading up to my fight in Europe told me that I would have to win by knockout or decisively dominate him to get the victory. Historically, I knew boxers rarely get wins by decision on their opponent's home turf.

Knowing the obstacles at hand, I put in extra work. Aside from jogging the cold, damp, and cloudy London streets, most of the third part of my training camp was at an East London gym. Outside the facility stood a statue of a boxer who suffered the same fate as Patrick Day.

Bradley Stone died from injuries sustained in a British title fight. This was also where Michael Watson trained before a fight against Chris Eubanks Sr. that left him paralyzed. Meeting up with author Don McRae, who wrote in depth about Watson, Eubanks, and Stone in one of his books I love, *Dark Trade*, put me in the mood to read more books while I was in London.

An idle mind is a dangerous one. That's why I always have to keep busy when I am outside of training camp. I usually don't get much idle time before a fight, but I had an abundance of it leading up to this one. My idle time provoked me to do abnormal activities during the third part of my training camp. I sparred 16 rounds in one day leading up to the fight and read several books while in London.

Josh and I had a civil build-up to our fight, but things began getting edgier every time we saw each other. He was the only opponent to get under my skin. Wanting to hurt my opponent is a natural desire. That feeling intensified during the fight's build-up when Josh touched my belts at the weigh-in and called me a wanker. I was far removed from my natural state, geographically and mentally.

I usually slip into war mode the day before the fight. War mode, for me, is like solitary confinement, which is taxing for a person's spirit and mental health. In London, I was in war mode for three weeks. Each night, I wished the fight was the following day.

...

The crowd was everything I expected, plus more. Roughly 20,000 people filled the seats of the O2 arena in London, England, hoping to see the fight of the year. This was deeper than a home versus away boxing match in the US.

253

My family, friends, and fans could make their presence felt at any arena in the United States. It would be impossible to get that effect in the O2 arena in London. They accounted for only 2% of the crowd and were spread throughout the arena instead of together as usual. Feeling the wrath of boos as I walked to the ring shook off my jitters and reminded me of what I was up against.

While Josh Taylor and I felt each other out after the opening bell, I began looking for my opportunity to hurt him. We quickly got the crowd involved and traded punches. The first three rounds felt like a tug-of-war. Two minutes into the third round, I landed an uppercut that would have electrified any neutral crowd. After his head snapped back, the crowd reserved their reaction for a harmless jab he landed moments later.

Crowds are an X-factor in boxing matches. All of Taylor's moves were met with excitement by the crowd. Scoring is subjective, and fans subconsciously influence the judges. Sometimes, it boils down to what the judges like. Some officials score rounds based on who is hurt the most, while others base it on who lands the most punches. I felt that I started the fight on top, and Josh began having a slight edge during some of the middle rounds.

A much-needed push came after the 8th round when one of my trainers, Hollywood, yelled, "Wake the fuck up! You don't want to give away all that hardware."

After I hurried out of the corner to start the 9th round, I rattled off a few thunderous blows the crowd didn't react to. Those punches would have sent any unbiased audience into a frenzy. Every punch Taylor landed or came close to landing provoked cheers. Once the crowd erupted after he swung at my shoulder and missed, I knew the only way I would win was by knockout. That didn't deter me from going for one.

I dominated the final rounds and regained control of the close fight. He was only a few punches away from dropping as he held on with a horrific eye injury and fought in survival mode during the closing minutes. Once the final round ended, an epiphany surfaced.

While the announcer prepared to reveal the scorecards, I committed to positively embracing the outcome either way. The first judge's score was 114 - 114. When the second judge's scorecard was read, it felt like someone punctured the air out of my tires. My undefeated streak officially ended when the third judge's scorecard was read. The entire arena erupted, but I didn't hear a thing.

It took me a moment to gather myself, but disrespecting the sport and not showing sportsmanship wasn't an option. Despite my feelings that I won the fight, Josh Taylor deserved that moment, along with my congratulations and respect. A champion must act like one during victory and defeat.

It's important to identify
the difference between
a sacrifice and a
compromise.

————————

LESSON

CHAPTER 27

~~Loss~~ Lessons

Thoughts of Patrick Day resurfaced while I was preparing to leave the arena. Ray asked, "Why didn't you duck more?" That was my first time smiling after the fight. My son's concern, love, and humor gave me foreshadowing of how I would get over my defeat.

Once I laughed, a pain riveted through my head. If Ray wasn't under my arm and Patrick Day hadn't passed away several days earlier, I am not sure I would have taken the precautions I did. As the pain surfaced, I asked to be brought to the hospital.

Patrick Day's tragic outcome put my loss in perspective. Even in his death, Day came out a victor. His name will live on forever in boxing, and his life will impact those outside the sport. Learning about Day's story made the situation even more complex.

Boxing is typically a poor man's sport, but Patrick Day's dad was a doctor, his mom had a high-paying career, and he had two degrees that could have helped him secure a high-paying job. Patrick Day didn't come from hard origins or need boxing like most fighters. Nonetheless, he forewent the safe route and put his life on the line for the sport we mutually love. The traumatic brain injury caused his death, but propelled him to immortality.

I know what I sacrifice to put on a show for the fans and do what I love. The life-risking sport makes me feel alive more than any activity. Having something to die for brings a new depth to living.

An undefeated record meant everything while having it, but I never attached my identity or legacy to my record. Before the Mayweather era, most fighters' primary purpose was to fight the best. Now, most fighters' main goal is to protect their 0 in the loss column.

The consequence of the best not facing the best has led to a decline in historic matches. By facing the best competition, I learned more from my defeat than what other boxers learn in one-sided matches where they aren't tested.

Momentarily, it felt like the end of the world when Taylor's hand was raised at the end of the match. Reading prepared me for the adversity I would be facing. I knew I was subject to modern-day boxing purgatory and would have to travel the hard road again to prove myself.

The most forgotten statistic and study in boxing is what happens to boxers after a defeat. The opponents I faced had a cumulative record of 51 wins and 128 losses after we shared the ring. Almost every boxer I faced went downhill after facing me.

Some fighters have the ability to damage others past their fights. Reflecting on what happened to my opponents after I faced them gave me an understanding of why many people didn't want to fight me. Also, it gave me insight into what I would have to overcome to make it back on top. Many boxers don't make it past their defeats.

A listing on the stock exchange can't crash as fast as a boxer's stock after losing a fight. However, I never let other people determine my value. Scrutiny was inevitable, but how my loved ones perceive me outweighs the perception of any analyst, fan, or social media user. My family and friends helped me recover from the loss before I went to sleep that night because they still treated me like a champion.

I gained reassurance in some unexpected places, also. Many people I bumped into after the fight in London felt that I won. Even the ones who agreed with the decision were still respectful and appreciative of the show I put on.

Counting my blessings minimized the negative impact of my loss. I gained an international fan base, made a lot of money, lived to fight another day, and learned valuable lessons to advance my career. There was nothing I could do to put the spilled milk back in the carton, but I made plans to never let it spill again.

Although I thought I would have gotten the decision on US soil, that didn't deter me from wanting to fight internationally again. The chance to represent my city in another country and impact people from different countries motivated me to continue displaying my talents worldwide.

The best time to implement a resolution isn't January 1st. It's when you realize something needs to change. I knew moving to California worked against me boxing-wise, so I began shopping for homes in Houston shortly after I returned to the States.

My corner and I had never been in this situation. We agreed that we left too early for London and talked about other things we could have done differently. The pep talk I received late in the fight should have happened during the mid-rounds, and we should have used sparring partners that mirrored my opponent's style. I overextended myself and entered uncharted territory before and during the fight.

I went longer than usual before rewatching my most recent fight. When I watched the life-changing match on my TV at home, I identified several areas of opportunity, but my stance on who won remained the same. The confirmation went from my soul to my eyes after seeing the statistics. Despite landing more punches and harder blows with more accuracy, I still didn't get the decision. That lit a fire under me, but there was nothing I could do about the fire aside from applying it to my future.

One of my biggest wins happened after the life-changing loss. It had always been a dream of mine to buy my mom a house. Weeks after the fight, I bought her one.

Dank started building houses around the same time I began boxing. He built a beautiful home I could see my mom living in. I thought the home-buying process would be easy because of the amount of funds I had, but it wasn't.

The process was an unexpected fight. I planned on buying it through the bank, but ended up paying cash for it. The amount of money I spent felt like a loss, but it was all worth it when I surprised my mom with a house on Christmas 2019.

For several days, I felt like I was on top of the world. Blessing my mom with a new house put me in the Christmas spirit. It seemed like I would be having a perfect break back home.

One week later, my mom called me with several concerns. Sometimes, our blessings are less enjoyable when we share them with the wrong people. My mom was initially excited about the house, but her happiness dwindled because of who she was surrounded by at the time. As we proceeded with the paperwork, she began speaking about secondhand worries and eventually turned down my gift.

I was at a loss for words when I was stuck with the property. I lived in Houston and had no intentions of moving back to New Orleans. The change of events pushed my emotional intelligence to the limit. I had to think quickly while riding a wave of chaotic emotions.

Boxing reminded me of its importance again that winter. The boxing gym was always the place that cleared my mind and gave me a place to let my frustrations out. Someone convincing my mom against her better judgment infuriated me, but there was nothing I could do about it aside from turning to my outlet. While letting my frustrations out hours before daybreak at the boxing gym, I reflected on doing the same thing as a teenager and how much boxing means to me.

The cards in the 140-pound division were shuffled after the tournament. Many boxers go into isolation after a defeat until they reappear for a tune-up fight to rebuild their confidence. Not being a world champion anymore made me appreciate the status all boxers strive for, but only a few get.

The road in my financial life may have been difficult as I climbed the ranks, but becoming a world champion in the ring came easy to me. Therefore, I didn't appreciate it as much as I should have. Missing the feeling of being a world champion reignited my hunger to reclaim my status.

I never considered going into isolation after my lone defeat. I had nothing to be ashamed of and needed to be active on the scene to position myself for another major fight. If you disappear after a loss in life, it'll be harder to find your next victory. One of the first events I attended after my fight with

Taylor was Mikey Garcia and Jessie Vargas's press conference in December 2019.

While there, I bumped into Eddie Hearn, the CEO of Matchroom. The son of the legendary promoter Barry Hearn had already begun carving out his own legacy in boxing. One year earlier, he signed boxing's first $1 billion deal when Matchroom and DAZN signed an agreement to stream boxing events across the US.

Quickly after greeting him, I pitched the idea of fighting the winner of Garcia and Vargas. Eddie responded, "I don't know about that, but how about fighting Maurice Hooker?" His boxing pedigree showed itself by matchmaking a fight that had been in the works for over a decade.

I faced Hooker in the amateurs, and we developed a little rivalry because we were fighting out of the same state and weight division. He started his career with a draw, then won 13 in a row until he scored another draw against Abel Ramos, who I defeated in the 8th round.

Hooker made a name for himself since becoming a professional. He was signed with Jay-Z's sports management company, Roc Nation. Our fight had been building up over the years and marinated for the perfect time.

We were coming off losses against the newly ranked #1 and #2 fighters in the division. Fighting each other brought danger.

Stakes in boxing don't get much higher than a fight where two boxers are at the crossroads.

Fighters whose livelihoods and careers are on the line can spark the same level of intensity as a world title match. He and I were one step away from the top and bottom. The winner would be back in the picture for a world title fight, and the loser would be further in the pits of boxing purgatory.

Initially, I thought the winner between Hooker, and I would be back in the front of the line for a belt in the 140-pound division. Having our fight at a catchweight in between two divisions pulled us away from that opportunity. Nonetheless, this was a fight I wanted and an opportunity to headline a pay-per-view card, earn seven figures, and settle a rivalry.

Boxing trash talk is the dirtiest of all sports, but there are unwritten rules regarding talking shit to another boxer. Maurice crossed that line several times throughout the promotion of our fight. Saying he would fight me in the streets and fabricating what happened during our fight in the amateurs made me want to put my hands on him even more. Talks for our fight became serious in January, and in February, we signed a deal to fight at the MGM National Harbor in Maryland on April 17, 2020, on DAZN.

It's important to identify the difference between a sacrifice and a compromise. Initially, he wanted us to fight at a catchweight of 143 lbs. A few pounds in boxing make a major

264

difference. My plan A exterminated any thoughts of a Plan B. I was locked in on becoming a 2x world champion and regaining my belts at 140.

Maurice already had his sights on moving up to the 147-pound division. He weighed in at 144 lbs.+ for his previous fight. We questioned each other's discipline to make weight. That was just a minor part of our back-and-forth trash talk on social media and to the press.

Another topic began dominating headlines in early 2020. A new decade delivered a new way of life. For 15 years, I thought there would never be a bigger life disruption than Hurricane Katrina. Returning to the ring was at the front of my mind to start the year, but it would have to go on the back burner due to the pandemic.

Sometimes, we go through situations to prepare us for our future blessings and opportunities. A countless number of times, I asked God, "Why did Hurricane Katrina happen?" My persistence in figuring out why I endured a tragedy led me to discover one of my biggest callings. Also, it prepared me for the COVID-19 pandemic.

Before the pandemic, I developed experience identifying blessings in the midst of adversity. Regardless of whether I had a fight coming up or not, Bobby and I worked together. Now, we were over 1,500 miles apart while I climbed to new heights in my career. Our bond was deeper than us working together.

The camaraderie, conversations, and connection we shared were missing elements.

The strength of connection often influences the strength of a boxer-trainer tandem. While sparring in LA, the connection between Julian Chua and his fighters was too strong to go unnoticed. His boxers exerted a different type of energy while he put them through innovative drills and poured his extensive knowledge into them. Julian's words are so influential that one of his fighters has a quote Julian said tattooed on his back.

A form of adversity helped him create an impactful moment in his career. The unthinkable happened when he traveled with one of his boxers for a match in another country. Imagine facing off with a boxer the day before you two are scheduled to fight, and then someone different showing up to fight you.

That's what happened to Julian's fighter on this trip. The person he was initially matched up with was underwhelming in stature and had a losing record. The face-off was the last time he saw that opponent. When he stepped into the ring the next day, a different and bigger opponent was waiting for him.

Julian's fighter's motivation wore off by the end of the third round during a four-round match. He performed well during the first round, but his poor performances in rounds two and three made his opening round an afterthought.

As he sat with his head down and shoulders slumped in the corner before the last round, Julian kneeled in front of him, then yelled, "Pick your head up, and don't feel sorry for yourself! We didn't come way out here to lose. Don't let anything get in between you and your goals. You chose this life!" Julian's fighter regained his steam from the first round and plowed through his opponent in the final round to get the victory.

I was confident about Julian's gift to train, motivate, and connect with his fighters before he told me that story. The timing of our connection reiterated the importance of it. Bobby had been my sole source of training since we connected, and most people at the highest level of boxing have multiple people to give them different looks in the ring.

I know my counterparts experienced the pandemic in different elements. Some saw it as an opportunity to take a break from the rigorous and grueling grind. Others had their hands full with lifestyle changes. I saw it as an opportunity to improve.

During the pandemic, Julian and I worked side-by-side, and I knew I wanted him on my team going forward. I'll forever appreciate that Julian took a chance to work with me while the world was still cautious about interacting closely with anyone. The world slowed down, but my grind didn't.

· · ·

There is danger in solely identifying as what you do professionally. Once that's taken away, what will remain?

Boxing is a significant part of my identity, but so is being a husband, father, son, uncle, friend, reader, entrepreneur, and adventurer. Everyone's profession experienced some type of disturbance due to the pandemic.

The life disruption reminded me of how thankful I am for my foundation. The extra time at home caused me to fall deeper in love with my wife and have more time to experience priceless moments with my family. Many people didn't get the luxury of enjoying their extra time at home, but I thoroughly enjoyed mine.

Spending more time with my children made me realize how my parenting style differs from my parents. They presented a structure and constant reminders that I was the child, and they were the parents. My parents came from two different types of households.

My mom came from loving and nurturing parents who spoiled her throughout adulthood. My maternal grandparents poured into my sister and me like they did my mother. My dad came from a chaotic home and vowed not to repeat that cycle. Regardless of their different upbringings, they were mostly on the same page with parenting India and me.

Discipline and respectfulness are non-negotiables for my kids, but I often carry on with them as if I am one of their siblings. Playing alongside them helps me bond with my kids at a deeper level and discover their differences.

One day during the pandemic, Ray and I were going back and forth while driving in the subdivision, and I joked with him that he would have to walk home. He acted as if that wouldn't be a problem. Once I got to a safe place in our neighborhood, I told him to get out.

I drove 5 mph down the street while looking at him in the rearview mirror. He looked unbothered and walked toward our house as if he was still riding in the back seat. If that was my daughter, Khalessi, she would have thrown a fit and cried up a storm. Ray's bravery put the biggest smile on my face. When he got back in the car, I made up for the joke by treating him to something special.

Almost every day after the pandemic started, I constantly checked my phone for notifications that restrictions would be lifted, and life would return to normal. While life was anything but normal, I did all I could to keep a sense of normalcy and continuity in my world. As winter turned into spring, Raquel and I planned our move back to the south. We found a house in Katy, Texas, and moved back in June 2020.

Maurice Hooker and I were scheduled to fight before the pandemic, but people were still excited to see our fight during lockdown. Things had already spilled out of the ring and got a tad bit personal.

My friends have the funniest way of making their presence felt during my career. Dank had already gone viral from verbally going at it with Terence Crawford before my first big fight in New Orleans. Somehow, he got Maurice Hooker's number. He held onto it for a while until Hooker began talking more noise about me online.

Shortly after moving back to Texas, Dank Facetimed me and asked me to hold on. I didn't know who he was Facetiming. The person answered in the dark. After the person spoke under their breath, Dank said, "Turn the light on!" as if he was talking to one of his kids like they were in trouble. After the lights were turned on, Maurice appeared on the other side of the screen.

Dank confronted him about the personal things he said about me, and I couldn't help but laugh. It was a funny moment and a reminder not to take things personally in the boxing world. I began losing faith that Hooker and I would ever share the ring.

Shortly after the three-way call, a story broke that Maurice Hooker would cancel our fight and move up a weight class. I wasn't surprised when he announced the news, but I thought it was the wrong step for his career. He was in the mix at the top in the 140-pound division, but would have further to climb in the 147-pound division.

Our fight would have been an opportunity to settle the odds, make a lot of money, and give the boxing world a fight they desired. Instead, our matchup went down as a potential classic fight that never happened. Letting fights marinate has been a great recipe for building up major fights, but letting them marinate for too long has been the main reason why many fights never take place.

My grind during the pandemic helped me realize that my feelings for boxing are deeper than love. I developed a passionate obsession for boxing. Whether people like to admit it or not, most forms of love come with conditions. Regardless of how much a person loves someone or something, love isn't always enough.

How many couples have loved each other, but love wasn't enough to keep them together? How many people have loved a sport, but didn't give it their all or make all the sacrifices possible to achieve their goals? An obsession is how most top performers of all disciplines identify their passion for their craft. Determining if you love your craft or if you are obsessed with it will influence your success at it. A person who loves their craft and a person who is obsessed with it are two different animals.

I always appreciated boxing fans, but
the pandemic helped me develop the ultimate
appreciation for them. As I watched boxing with
no fans in the seats, I was alarmed at how much
was missing from the sport.

————————

LESSON

CHAPTER 28

Grief & Gratitude

The saying, "As a person leaves this world, a child is born," hit home in 2020. Within a week of finding out my wife was pregnant with our third child, Khalanni, I received heartbreaking news that my grandfather would be dying soon. Watching my third child grow in my wife's stomach while my grandfather transitioned humbled me to pieces. My grandfather's oldest brother, Uncle Jesse, also passed away within this timeframe.

Being well-read provides you with a mental bank account you can make everlasting withdrawals from. A history lesson showed me how grief can empower a fighter. In 1990, almost no one on earth predicted Buster Douglas would have a chance at beating Mike Tyson.

At the time, Tyson was the undisputed heavyweight champion, in his prime, and knocked out his first 18 opponents. Douglas was one of the biggest underdogs in sports betting history. A few more people might have placed a bet on him if they knew about his mother's dying wish.

Shortly before his mother passed away, she told him he would beat Mike Tyson. She died before getting the opportunity to watch her son make history and see her prophecy come to life.

Have you ever seen supernatural strength in motion, like when a mother utilizes her strength to protect her child, or someone exerts self-preservation efforts? A person's purpose will influence their powers or lack thereof.

Buster Douglas's purpose helped him pull off one of the biggest upsets in sports history. Mike Tyson had a Hall-of-Fame career and changed the sport of boxing. However, none of that mattered during that night in history. Buster Douglas's purpose of fulfilling his mother's premonition was what mattered the most.

My next fight would be dedicated to my late grandfather and soon-to-be-born baby girl. This would be the first pro fight my grandfather ever missed and the first boxing match with fans after the pandemic. It was unimaginable in several ways. My fight against Juan Heraldez was scheduled in San Antonio on Halloween night, one year since my last fight, and one day after my wife's due date.

I wasn't surprised that I had to fight on a holiday and potentially miss my child's birth. The surprise was that my return to the ring came on an undercard. I was a former world champion and ranked #1 in my division for several years, but my only opportunity to fight was on an undercard in a slot usually reserved for prospects.

My opponent and his team began buying into the doubters when facing me. Each person I fought before Heraldez was respectful of my skills in the ring. Videos began surfacing of his team talking down on me. He brought the same trash he talked on Twitter into our press conference.

I knew Heraldez wasn't on my level, but he made me want to remind him of that. An ulterior motive for taking this fight was positioning myself to secure a major fight. It was rumored that Mario Barrios, or I would get a chance to fight Gervonta Davis next. Davis was headlining the event against Leo Santa Cruz.

The press conference was different from anything I ever experienced. We were placed on opposite sides of the stage, with the mediator in the middle. Our face-off would have to be from a distance.

Usually, I could look into someone's eyes and see where their heart and head are. From across the stage, I sensed his illusion of what would occur once we got in the ring. He tried convincing himself and everyone listening that my time at the top was over, and now it was his turn.

The reasons for motivation were stacked to the ceiling for my fight at the Alamodome in San Antonio. My wife's water could break at any moment. My grandfather and great-uncle passed away right before the fight, I felt slighted about being on an undercard, and I wanted to give spectators a tremendous showing on the first televised fight with fans in attendance since the suspension of all the fights.

I always appreciated boxing fans, but the pandemic helped me develop the ultimate appreciation for them. As I watched boxing with no fans in the seats, I was alarmed by how much was missing from the sport. Punches that typically thrilled the crowd echoed in the empty arenas. I hoped I would have fans to perform in front of when I returned to the ring, and I was thankful for the opportunity.

...

If my wife gave birth to Khalanni before the fight, I would have missed it because I was restricted to a bubble in San Antonio for the boxing match. I try to stay away from my phone leading up to fights, but I kept checking it while my youngest daughter was inching her way into the world. My family remained on my mind more than ever leading up to the fight. Most of my family was still grieving my grandpa and Uncle Jessie while anticipating a new addition.

A video on YouTube the night before the fight made me put my phone down and channel my energy. Typically, I'd lose a few pounds a day on Mondays and Tuesdays before my fights. We'd been in the bubble on Tuesday, and I was out of my typical fight routine for one year leading up to my first fight since the pandemic started. That played a factor in missing weight, but no excuses were justifiable. Not making weight gave Heraldez and his team another rag to chew on. They continued their disrespect the night before the fight.

An interviewer asked Juan and his trainer, "How did Regis look at the weigh-in?"

After saying a few lines not worth quoting, Juan answered, "It looked like he was dying up there."

Then his trainer added, "Like a bitch," and went on to say my skills were low and that Juan would take me to the deep waters and drown me.

Regardless of the circumstances before the fight, I felt the opposite of how I did one year before my fight in London. I was relaxed in war mode and fighting only a few hours away from my second home. It was a struggle to suppress my emotions about my grandfather not being able to see me fight again in person, but I knew he would be watching from Heaven.

More than 14,000 fans showed up on Halloween night to attend the first boxing match open to fans since the pandemic. My polar feelings of grief and gratitude gave me a sense of urgency as I walked to the ring in my fighting costume.

While the announcer announced my record with a loss for the first time, the fire reignited inside me. Juan Heraldez was coming off an upset victory against another southpaw fighter. His backing from Mayweather promotions also boosted his confidence.

This was one of the first fights I entered the ring with a game plan. I wanted to put him on his back as quickly and disrespectfully as possible. As I walked to the ring, my wife could have been going into labor. I needed to get back to my family as soon as possible.

Quickly into the first round, I gained confirmation that he and I weren't on the same level. My head swiftly swiveled side-to-side throughout the beginning of the first round. I threw hard jabs and searched for my opening.

As my jab got comfortable on his forehead and I found a home for my left hand, I realized that this fight wasn't worth boxing. Almost every punch I threw had bad intentions. I had an answer for every punch he occasionally threw, and he didn't have an answer for my left hand.

Halfway through the first round, I set him up for an overhand left. Once I connected, I couldn't keep my left hand off him. I spent the rest of the round punishing him with it and walking him down as he backpedaled and tried fighting me off him.

The second stanza was target practice for me. It's one thing to hit your target, but it's another thing to punch through it. My opponent did me a favor after the opening round by throwing more punches. I was able to pick up on everything he did. I knew what he was going to do before he did it.

My adversary overextended after every combination he threw and kept leaving his right hand down. He had no answer for my left. I stared into his eyes at the beginning of the third round and saw that he didn't believe the shit he talked leading up to the fight. My opponent looked like a defeated fighter before our fight was over.

Shit-talking is a part of boxing, so I didn't take his down-talking of me personally, but he had to be taught a lesson. My opponent threw a careless two-punch combination that wouldn't have done any damage if they landed. After the two missed punches, his body was awkwardly twisted, and his chin looked like a baseball sitting across the middle of the plate.

While his chin was exposed, I cocked back and swept him off his feet with an overhand left. I knew the fight was only moments away from ending when I saw the confusion on his face as the punch propelled him into the air. The fight was over seconds after the first knockdown, and I was officially back once the ref waved off the fight.

It's easy to misconceive that boxers dislike their opponents when they talk trash before fights. However, that's a common misconception about boxing. A fighter shouldn't have strict boundaries on what they need to tell themselves to build their confidence and sell the fight. A fight is naturally more intriguing when there is bad blood. Promoters often fabricate or cultivate a beef between fighters to make the fight more intriguing.

My beef with Juan Heraldez ended after I dropped him for the first time. I knew he would return to the fight defenseless and that I didn't have any hard feelings toward him. After our bout, I thanked my opponent for the fight and wished him the best of luck going forward.

I usually bask in all aspects of my post-fight victories, such as the post-fight interview in the ring, calling out other fighters, and speaking with the media. When the fight ended, I rushed through all my post-fight obligations to check on Raquel and the baby. I tasted the ultimate happiness when I found out my wife hadn't gone into labor yet. It felt like God was ordering my footsteps every step of the way, even in the lowest times.

Things worked out better than I planned. Initially, I thought I would have to get on the road after the fight and drive east for a few hours. I didn't get touched that night and had the energy to drive back, but I needed the rest mentally and emotionally. Instead of getting on the road after the fight, I spent the rest of the night surrounded by family and friends at an Airbnb in the suburbs of San Antonio.

Khalanni's birth was the symbol of a new beginning. It was as if my grandfather, Raquel, and God were working together to mend the pain of his passing and give Khalanni a perfect welcome to this world. The following morning, I got on the road back home to witness Khalanni's birth. I was still worn out when I returned home. Surprisingly, I had enough time to get some sleep. Raquel told me to take a nap. Two hours later, she woke me up to inform me that Khalanni was on the way.

Planning a homebirth worked in my favor better than I could have imagined. Instead of driving thirty minutes to a doctor's office and hanging around there for a few days, I called the midwife over, and my wife would have the opportunity to recover at home. Moments before childbirth are more nerve-racking than the moments before a fight. In a fight, I have control over the experience, but I had to relinquish control to my wife, the midwife, and God as Raquel prepared to give birth.

When the dust settled after my victory against Heraldez, and real life picked back up after Khalanni's birth, I learned that adversity doesn't have a dollar sign. I still felt the pain of grief and being overlooked, regardless of how much I progressed financially. My reputation of being a high-risk, low-reward fight increased when I wasn't a title holder. I was used to people ducking me, but I was not used to people questioning my skills.

My debatable loss provoked a new set of critics and a new form of criticism. Heraldez was the first opponent to question my skills. I captioned his knockout on Instagram, "Put some fucking respect on my name." It was a viral quote from the New Orleans mogul, Brian Birdman Williams, during a Breakfast Club interview, but that was how I felt at the time.

They say time is not on our side, but the
odds of it being on our side increase when
we use our time wisely.

———————

LESSON

CHAPTER 29

Boxing Purgatory

I f we don't take chances, we'll have to accept the circumstances at hand. Not one potential fight materialized throughout the rest of 2020 and the beginning of 2021. Having another year-long layoff, which can be detrimental to a boxer, wasn't ideal.

The belts were tied up at the time. Josh Taylor and Jose Ramirez held all the belts in the 140-pound division, and they were scheduled to fight to become the undisputed champion on May 22, 2021. Without a shot at getting a title in my next fight, I decided to take a chance.

While proving myself on ShoBox in 2015, Triller was created. Our careers intersected during the Spring of 2021. The Triller app was originally designed as a video editor but graduated to social media and sports events.

Triller reached out to me to partake in the first professional fight on their platform at the turn of 2021. It was a no-brainer for me but a headscratcher for some. Fighting on Triller's platform gave me the opportunity to tap into a new fanbase, expose my talents to an audience outside of the boxing world, and earn a lucrative payday.

Fighting on a non-traditional boxing card drew a lot of criticism from many people in the boxing world, but I wasn't a stranger to it, so I didn't let it affect me. Performing on a new platform provided me with a new form of excitement. The typical press conference for a fight consists of boxing legends, boxing media, and family and friends of the boxers. At the press conference in Las Vegas, I came across stars from all disciplines and experienced some occurrences in boxing I never envisioned. My motivation was through the roof when I returned to Houston. When I made it home, I put on my boots and ran 10 miles to prepare for the task at hand.

When I spar outside of camp, I try anything in the ring, especially if I am boxing against a guy not on my level. Ivan Redkach and I sparred at Churchill Gym one year before we faced each other in an official match. After a few minutes of sparring Ivan, I was unimpressed and began trying anything against him. He landed a few harmless hits against me while I played around with him. When we finished and shook hands, I thought that day would be placed in the vault of sparring days.

Quickly into promoting our fight, Ivan began telling reporters that he battered me during sparring and had my nose bloody. I knew I would make easy work of him. The hard work came outside the ring preparing for him.

We fought at a catchweight of 142 lbs., and I had a hard time making weight again. Bobby had a portable sauna, and I sat in there along with my other normal methods of cutting weight, but I still couldn't get down to 140 lbs. I weighed in at 143.5 lbs. Becoming a two-time world champion at 140 appeared less promising than ever when I fought on an undercard of a non-traditional boxing event and weighed in at my heaviest weight ever.

The passing of one of my favorite idols, Marvin Hagler, before the fight brought sadness and focus to my world. Being from New Orleans, an avid reader, and experiencing a unique path in life makes it hard for me to identify with other current and retired boxers. However, Marvin Hagler stands out to me as someone whose career was most like mine.

Hagler's career epitomized the hard road. I took the hard road as well. The challenges he overcame in the boxing world inspired me to overcome my own. I felt far away from my goals during the time of his passing, but after his death, I was inspired to progress closer to them.

My fight against Ivan went as expected, but did not end as expected. I dominated him in the first five rounds and felt a knockout coming soon, like everyone else watching the fight. Snoop Dogg broadcasted the fight and said Ivan's body was open all night like a 7-Eleven.

During the sixth round, I landed 11 power punches. The 11th was a right hook to the body that dropped Ivan to his knees and made him put on a show like I never saw before. He cried and rolled over like a hurt toddler looking for sympathy to avoid punishment for something they shouldn't have done. A ring physician checked on him, and minutes later, he was carried away from the ring on a stretcher.

He was looking for a way out of the fight and thought he found one by pretending that I hit him below the belt. If this fight was before the technology of instant replay, people would have still been able to tell he was faking it by his antics after taking a legal body shot. He flopped around the ring like a fish with no water.

The initial controversy was resolved when the replay was shown on the jumbotrons for everyone to see. People instantly grew irate about him quitting the match and taking a shameful way out. Despite the outrage, the referee scored it a TKO, and I won due to the score on the cards rather than a knockout. I busted my ass to prepare for this fight and earned a knockout, so I refused to settle for less than what I deserved. I immediately appealed the decision and was infuriated in the meantime. I deserved my credit after the fight and was robbed of it because of a sore loser.

While unable to fully enjoy my victory, I thought about the late legend who inspired me to remain persistent before the fight. Marvin Hagler wasn't able to enjoy his first title victory because the fans threw alcoholic beverages into the ring and vandalized the arena once he won. Shortly after his passing, I decided to get his picture tattooed on my arm next to Muhammad Ali.

I dreamed about being able to learn from Hagler in person. He moved to Europe and began a new life after he retired from boxing in 1987. Because of my extensive research on him, I felt like I already knew him when we met in 2014 at a boxing convention. Not having the opportunity to learn from him in person motivated me to learn from as many boxing legends as possible. I would get the opportunity to learn from two of my favorite boxing idols before my next fight.

A few months before fighting on Triller, I Facetimed Roy Jones. He gave me some valuable boxing gems, a heads-up about how things worked with Triller, and an invitation to train with him. The opportunity meant the world to me. It was a surreal experience to build a relationship with someone I grew up idolizing. When we Facetimed, he advised me to throw fewer power punches to catch my opponents off guard. I implemented the short and spontaneous advice and saw immediate improvement. That made me hungry to learn more from him.

In June of 2021, I traveled to Pensacola, Florida, to train with Roy Jones Jr. He was living the kind of life I would consider after retirement. Roy had a training facility on plenty of acres detached from society and the bright lights he shined under during his Hall-of-Fame career. He preferred to be surrounded by his animals and land instead of city life. Chickens even walked in the ring while I trained. I didn't have a list of things I wanted to learn from Roy. It was more about the experience and relationship for me.

His mindset was one of my biggest takeaways. Most gifted athletes love to boast about themselves, but Roy gave all the glory to God. He said that he was just blessed with the opportunity to show the world his God-given gifts. Learning from him in person gave me a chance to learn past misperceptions and understand what made a Hall-of-Fame fighter legendary.

The boxing world often feels like a society within society. Even avid boxing fans have distorted perceptions of what goes on behind the scenes and the nuances of the boxing world. Losing the person who formally introduced me to the boxing world, and another boxing-related death alluded to the dark times during boxing purgatory.

Coach Willie Savannah's passing in 2020 put a cloud over the Houston boxing world and affected a countless number of people including myself. I'll always be thankful for the contributions he made to my career. Coach Savannah eased my transition to becoming a boxer and adapting to life after Hurricane Katrina.

It's easy to assume I'm the toughest person in my corner, but March 11, 2021, showed me that I have one of the toughest people on Earth in my corner. My cutman, Aaron Navarro, boxed as an amateur and continued hanging around the boxing gym after he decided not to pursue a pro career. Boxing is in his bloodline. His grandfather was a boxer. Hanging around the gym helped him find a new career in the boxing realm.

Aaron had a connection with New Orleans before I was born. Walt Haley, the first trainer he worked under, was from New Orleans. Haley trained several New Orleans boxing legends, including Ralph Dupas, Willie Pastrano, and Tiffany Juno, the first female world champion from New Orleans.

Aaron has the personality to make you feel like you've known him long before you met him. Several years into the apprentice phase of his career, he teamed with Bobby and began training his own boxers. Bobby and Aaron had been working together for two decades before I came along.

On March 11, 2021, Aaron experienced a tragedy that no human on earth should be subjected to. That night, he lost his daughter Angela "Birdie" Navarro to a domestic dispute. The numbing pain of when I first got the news still reoccurs as I recall the occurrence years later. Death is an inevitable fate for all of us, but this loss altered my view of it.

Our lives and actions are deeper than us. The man responsible for her death didn't only affect the people in the dispute, he affected hundreds at Angela's vigil. Everyone in the gym showed up to support Aaron and pay our respects to Angela.

Her rest in peace shirt would connect us forever. The picture used to memorialize Angela was a picture of her wearing a t-shirt with my picture on it. That was deeper than any memory she and I could have shared.

Aaron felt more pain than anyone at the memorial, but held it together the strongest. That strength carried on to his everyday life. He was back at the gym before most of the gym members that attended the memorial.

...

No other fights materialized throughout 2021, but I was still making progress during the downtime. Aside from staying in shape, I addressed my biggest area of opportunity - making weight. Twitter seemed to be a launching pad for suggestions or questions, so I tweeted, "Does anyone know a good nutritionist I could hire?"

A wide range of people reached out to me, ranging from people who looked like they needed a nutritionist themselves to high-level nutritionists. The first person I contacted was a nutritionist in the UK who had experience with professional athletes. I knew the chances of finding someone local and suitable for the job were slim, but the UK was further than I anticipated.

The second person I came across was Declan Walsh, an award-winning Sports Nutritionist from Ireland and based in Canada. He worked with many elite boxers and UFC fighters and offered to travel to Houston for a mock training camp.

Declan stayed at my house when he traveled to Houston and switched up my food intake. Most importantly, he helped me understand what works for me and what works against me. I was doing things the wrong way. Soda, fast food, and junk food were a major part of my intake.

Declan and my team worked cohesively to put me through a mock training camp to test his process. In two weeks, I went from 158 lbs. to 139 lbs. and didn't feel the side effects I typically felt after cutting weight. He officially became part of my team after the mock training camp.

I thought I would need his services again sooner, but no fights materialized during the fall of 2021. There was no fight in the world worth sacrificing the experience that took place in November. While in New Orleans, a friend called me and said Roberto Duran was in town and wanted to connect with me.

Of all the ways I dreamed of meeting my favorite fighter, this was not how I envisioned it. I pictured bumping into him at a boxing event or approaching him as a fan. I couldn't help but approach a fighter on my Mount Rushmore as a fan. Contrary to my imagination, we met in an organic way to build a relationship.

I took him to lunch and spent time with him at the boxing gym. Learning priceless lessons from someone I idolize was a dream come true. He embodied every bit of the legendary fighter he is. As he showed me different tricks of the trade, he showed me that his instincts, tenacity, and quickness were still there. We did a stare-off, and I saw that he was more ready to fight in his 70s than most opponents I faced.

Things were back on the right track to reclaim my position at the top. I signed a promotional deal with Probellum, hired a nutritionist, and spent time with two legends. I was thankful for the value Lou DiBella provided for my career and that we were able to end our deal early. I reached a point in my career where I wanted to try new strategies to advance my career inside and outside the ring.

Probellum outbid the other promotional companies and sold me on the opportunity to fight across the world and get a world title shot within my first two fights with them. They fulfilled the first step of the promise and made headway on the second one by scheduling a fight in Dubai on March 19, 2022.

I would be facing Tyrone McKenna for a title eliminator. One month before my fight against McKenna, Josh Taylor planned on defending his belts against Jack Catterall. Taylor was heavily favored. Tyrone McKenna had just lost a close unanimous decision to Jack Catterall.

The dynamics in the 140-pound division appeared to be shifting again soon. Taylor consistently spoke about moving up a weight class, and several stars from the 135-pound division were talking about moving up to 140. With the help of a nutritionist, I extended my staying power in the 140-pound division.

My vision shifted. I envisioned being like Marvin Hagler and dominating one division instead of moving up another weight class. If I wouldn't have invested in myself, I would have tricked myself out of my position.

I decided to double down on investing in myself when buying a new house. Each house before this one was a short-term situation. Since I planned on being here long-term, I went about it differently. I built a gym in my backyard that included a ring, workout equipment, a basketball court, and everything I needed to work on my craft whenever I wanted to.

I didn't know who Tyrone McKenna was until he had something to say about my fight against Taylor. I thought he was a boxing fan talking trash to me on Twitter, but he was in the same profession and weight class as me. The fighter from Belfast, Northern Ireland, had a lot to say, and I didn't have any fights in the works, so I extended the olive branch for a fight. His people and mine made it work.

My morale was higher heading into my fight in Dubai than my three previous fights. After easily making weight against

McKenna, it felt like I was headed in the right direction. Sacrificing and investing in myself paid off again. Adjusting my food intake and hiring professional help weren't cheap or easy, but the extra effort and sacrifices were worth it. Sometimes, we should focus on the value of what we are paying for instead of the price.

Everyone outside my team expected me to miss weight, but I weighed in at 138.6 lbs. That gratifying personal victory brightened my future at 140. We all laughed when Benji joked that I might start fighting at 135, but I instantly thought about how I just regained control of my career.

Tyrone and I may have started on the wrong foot, but he became one of the most likable guys I ever fought. McKenna approached the fight as if he were adding a new opponent to his record and a new friend to his life. He joked that he planned on winning the fight by me hurting my hand on his head. I put on a boxing clinic against him and beat him up badly, but he kept encouraging me to hit him.

When I knocked him down with one of the fastest one-twos I ever threw, he raised his eyebrows and gave me a thumbs up. He tried fighting back as blood leaked from several areas of his face and spread across the ring. The ref stepped in to stop the onslaught in the 6th round.

Tyrone's prediction about me hurting my hand on his head was correct. After my hand healed, I was back training. Several big fights took place at the turn of 2022, but none impacted me more than Josh Taylor's fight against Jack Catterall.

Not many people outside of Catterall's camp expected a close fight, but he put on an impressive performance and knocked Taylor down in the 8th round. Once the fight ended, the announcers assumed there would be a new undisputed champion. After knocking Taylor down and outlanding him, Catterall wasn't announced the winner. When Josh said there wouldn't be a rematch, I wasn't sure of that statement. His desire to clear things up against Catterall became a priority before moving up a weight class and retaining his status as undisputed champion.

Being a world champion is like becoming an employee to the belt. The champion has a job to defend their belt and obligations to maintain it. The WBA ordered a mandatory bout between Josh Taylor and Alberto Puello. They had a 30-day negotiation period, starting in March, but the fight was never made.

Dynamics in the 140-pound division shifted in May when Josh Taylor no longer held the WBA belt. Several days later, news broke that the WBA would arrange a call with the top six contenders in the 140-pound division. Each would get 15 minutes to explain why they should fight for the vacant title. I knew Albert Puello would be a shoo-in because he was already scheduled to fight Taylor. I assumed I was the other shoo-in because I was the only former world champion in the running and previously held the WBA belt.

I went through many dark moments in boxing purgatory. One of the most painful moments in the darkness was when the WBA announced how they would proceed for the vacant title fight. Batyr Akhmedov, a Russian boxer with a 9-1 record, was selected to fight for the vacant title. They chose him over me, and four boxers ranked above him with more experience, wins, and accolades.

Not being selected to fight for the title wasn't the most disheartening news. I was named as a "substitute opponent" for a series of fights ordered by the WBA. The most qualified was the odd man out. I tried keeping my cool about being overlooked for a title shot until the following month.

When July rolled around, Josh relinquished the WBC title after three delayed purse bids. He made another attempt to pursue a rematch with Catterall and wished Jose Ramirez and Jose Zepeda good luck in the fight for his vacated WBC belt. Jose Ramirez fought once since his loss to Taylor, and I fought three times, but he was back in line before me.

Most men are taught to conceal their emotions, but I couldn't hold back from expressing them after being overlooked again. It wasn't just about being overlooked at that moment. It had been a recurring theme, but that repetitiveness sharpened the chip on my shoulder.

I was in a vulnerable position, but there is strength in vulnerability. At this point, others could see I was overlooked. The chip on my shoulder wouldn't let me settle for being overlooked and underrated. I wanted my just due.

I saw time differently from others on the outside looking in. They say time is not on our side, but the odds of it being on our side increase when we use our time wisely. Being locked out of a title shot gave me more time to get dangerous. I decided to put my head down, work, and not worry about what I couldn't control.

It's always better to be proactive than reactive. I wasn't sitting around waiting for something to happen while left in limbo. I had another fight scheduled for late August against Viktor Postol or Ricky Burns in Saudi Arabia. I kept those negotiations quiet in case an opportunity arose to fight for a belt.

Whispers began getting louder that Jose Ramirez would back out of the fight against Zepeda. I had already been on an emotional roller coaster, so I didn't get emotionally invested in the rumor.

On July 31, Ramirez officially turned down the fight. The WBC named me as Zepeda's opponent for the vacant title. Zepeda had two "knockout of the year" type knockouts two years in a row against quality opponents Ivan Barancyk and

Josue Vargas. Opportunity met preparation. This was the opportunity I prepared for while in boxing purgatory.

I was under the weather when I got the news, but I still had the motivation to train after taking several interviews on August 1. I was halfway into a training camp for a fight that didn't take place, and had minimal downtime before preparing for Zepeda, so I traveled to Colombia to detach momentarily.

My family grew accustomed to me missing important days, and it looked like I'd be missing another special date. My wife's birthday is on September 11, and I had a broadcasting opportunity in California on the tenth. We planned to have a delayed birthday celebration, but I had other plans.

Because of the business opportunity and conflicting schedules, Raquel and her friends went to Atlanta to celebrate. I flew to Georgia on the evening of Raquel's birthday and her friends hid me in a closet until they left for the club. I headed to the venue shortly thereafter and sent some bottles to their section when I made it there. Once the bottles arrived, I emerged from a secluded area with flowers in my hand. The smile on her face and happiness in her heart when we hugged made me feel that all the sacrifices we made together were worth it. I had to accomplish what I told her and myself I would.

Becoming the first at something opens doors for others to follow in the same footsteps. The pioneer always has the toughest path, but the struggles and challenges aren't in vain.

———————

LESSON

CHAPTER 30

Pioneer

Training camp in New Orleans was more for mental preparation than physical preparation. New Orleans nor the state of Louisiana has ever produced a two-time world champion. That would be part of my motivation to spend two weeks of training camp in New Orleans for the first time. There isn't a place in the world that could have provided me with a deeper sense of motivation.

I spent time hanging with loved ones and taking care of personal business during that part of training camp. Those activities kept me from being burnt out due to preparation for a fight that never happened. As I drove the streets of New Orleans to check on investment properties, I visualized younger me fighting on those same streets. I thought to myself, *I'm about to become the first two-time world champion from New Orleans.* The déjà vu reality helped me see how far I made it, but I knew I still had further to go and more to accomplish.

I knew there were other goals I wanted to achieve going forward, but this was one of the most meaningful. Becoming the first at something opens doors for others to follow in the same footsteps. The pioneer always has the toughest path, but the struggles and challenges aren't in vain. People who follow the path will have the opportunity to learn from the pioneer's mistakes and avoid unforeseen obstacles. I didn't have a blueprint or pioneer to follow, so I decided to show others a blueprint by becoming the pioneer. Doing so would provide hope to kids who walked in my shoes.

It was heartwarming to spend time with elders in the community and bring out people of all ages. My efforts were all worth it when I looked into the eyes of kids at the media workout. When most of them first walked in, I saw the look of uncertainty on their faces. These faces were searching for a way out and something to propel them past their current circumstances. Growing up, I had that same look in my eyes. Now, I had the power to enhance their visions and show them a way out.

As much as I love New Orleans, Houston became my boxing home, and it was time to return. If I lived back home in New Orleans as an adult, I know it would have hampered my boxing career. It was time to return to my natural boxing element, where I could grind and inspire my city the most.

. . .

Marv Nation outbid every promotional company for promotional rights to my fight with Zepeda. It's rare that a promoter with minimal experience in boxing gets promotional rights to a major fight, let alone a world title fight. Many boxing traditionalists were skeptical. It wasn't necessarily the amount of money they bid that mainly caught critics' attention. It was their strategy. They bid $2.4 million, and several other promotional companies bid slightly more than $1 million.

My fight, scheduled for November 26 in California, was one of the last major boxing events of 2022. Having one of the last championship fights of the year put pressure on the event to do well. That boiled down to more than Marv Nation, Jose Zepeda, and me. How entertaining the event would be dependent on the undercard also.

When I headline events, it's always a goal of mine to put as many fighters on the undercard as possible. I helped several friends and sparring partners get on the undercards in Dubai and London. Aside from advancing their careers, they were able to see the world and gain new fans internationally. Looking out for others also came with an advantage. Most likely, their fans would cheer for me when the main event rolled around. I tried getting several sparring partners on the undercard for my fight against Zepeda, but to no avail. That minimized my support in the arena. I didn't know one boxer on the undercard, but I heard about some of them.

One of them was connected to me in ways I didn't like thinking about. Charles Conwell and I never met, but the dates of our boxing careers crossed paths. On the day of my fight with Josh Taylor, Conwell's recent opponent, Patrick Day, was buried. Their fight will always stick with me because of the timing and the outcome. It was a suppressed memory that resurfaced.

His fight with Day showed the importance of 50/50 fights and symbolized a bigger problem - fights not being stopped in time. It's common for boxers of higher tiers to fight boxers of lower tiers. The B-side fighter is expected to lose. Losing in boxing is different from losing in non-combat sports.

Losing in boxing involves inevitable injuries such as a broken jaw, bloody nose, head trauma, and damaged body parts. The more uneven the fight, the more likely these injuries will happen. That's an underlying reason why 50/50 fights and my bout against Zepeda were important. More matchups like this were needed in the sport.

Conwell's fight on my undercard was against Juan Carlos Abreau, a fighter from the Dominican Republic. The rest of the card consisted of potential star power, including Bkhodir Jalovo, who already generated an extensive fan base of 1+ million followers on Instagram. He was fighting someone who generated a lot of traction on social media for reasons other than his boxing skills.

Curtis Harper went viral a year earlier when he faced Efe Ajagba in a heavyweight championship fight. Seconds after they touched gloves and the bell rang for the first round, Harper turned around and exited the ring. The scrutiny of his actions created a demeaning storyline that his abrupt exit was due to fear. Rushing to judge is the quickest direction away from the truth.

While the camera followed Harper for a lengthy walk down an elevated ramp and back to the dressing room, no one considered why he walked out of the ring. Business negotiations between the fighter and promoter went left, and Harper exited the ring as a form of protest. His reasoning should not be swept under the rug. Fighters face all types of challenges behind the scenes during their career and rarely get the chance to tell their side of the story.

The rest of the undercard consisted of Fernando Vargas's three sons - Fernando Vargas Jr., Amad Vargas, and Emiliano Vargas, Yokasta Valle, who was attempting to become a 5x world champion in three weight divisions of women's boxing, plus several other talented prospects and contenders.

Lessons of patience, business, and faith came into play when securing the Zepeda fight. Sometimes, chasing money can lead us further away from our destiny. If I was focused on chasing money, I would have signed the deal to fight in Saudi Arabia and would have only added to my bank account instead of my legacy. Fighting for the WBC world title gave me an opportunity to do both. It was time to apply those lessons further when I left New Orleans for the second part of my training camp in Houston.

Going through preparation for the potential fight in Saudi Arabia had me ahead of schedule when it was time for my training camp against Zepeda. The beginning of camp was running like a well-oiled machine. Everyone on my team knew what they were supposed to be doing, when they were supposed to be doing it, where they were supposed to be doing it, and how they were supposed to be doing it.

Monday mornings started in Downtown Houston at Main Street Boxing Gym. I would arrive after the morning rush of downtown traffic and talk with my team while stretching and warming up. The grind would start with sparring for ten rounds and drills in the ring. Immediately after sparring, I did strength and conditioning drills with Evins. It's one thing to train, but it's another thing to train after sparring for ten rounds. In between rounds were my only rest periods. Evins superset every strength and conditioning drill, with me throwing punches on the heavy bag.

After my first workout of training camp with Evins, I stuck my head out of a window the size of a shoebox on the second floor. While the wind chilled my fully opened pores, I knew this was about to be one of the longest training camps ever. I was already five weeks into a training camp for Postol or Burns, but now I was at the beginning of another training camp for the biggest fight of my career.

When I retracted my head back into the gym, the heat resurfaced on my face, and my team was heading downstairs for the third part of my workout. Bobby and I had more drills to do downstairs, including ab work and neck strengthening. This was the only fun part of my workout. I'd talk with Bobby, Benji, Evins, and Ross, my childhood friend and writer, while Bobby put me through drills. It still took a lot to fight through the final set of drills, but I knew the end of my workout was near.

The final workout of the day was several hours away. After a nap and brief time with my family, it was time to train in my ring. On Tuesdays, I worked out at home twice a day with Bobby and did pool work with Evins. Wednesdays mimicked Mondays. On Thursdays, we ran stairs and sparred in the sand. A break didn't come until Sunday because I hosted camp on Friday mornings and ran at the track with Evins on Saturday. After my first week of training camp in Houston, I was convinced Zepeda wasn't working as hard as me.

A storm led me to my calling,
so I embrace all storms
that come my way.

———

LESSON

CHAPTER 31

The Calm Before The Storm

Holidays are intricate parts of cultures worldwide. The energy in the atmosphere shifts during the holiday season. Kids and students are looking forward to long-awaited breaks. Adults hustle to make ends meet and spend time with their loved ones. Most businesses are shut down, and introverts embrace solitude.

Due to my boxing career, holidays are typically just another day on the calendar for me. I celebrate them when I have time, but I'm usually not granted the opportunity because I'm either fighting or preparing for one. During Thanksgiving week, I was focused on creating my own holiday.

Zepeda and I showed mutual respect and complemented one another when interviewed by the media leading up to the fight. Most guys who are heavy on the words or try the tough guy act are unsure of themselves or doing anything they can to get a mental advantage in the ring. I was sure of myself. There was no need to go back and forth with my opponent. I was here to do a job and didn't need extra incentives.

This was my first time as the main event since my fight against Taylor. Being on undercards after all I accomplished was the most disrespected and overlooked, I ever felt in my career. It was as if the boxing world threw me away after one blemish on my record. Being mistreated after a loss is a common dynamic in life. Taking a loss has positioned many people to achieve their greatest wins.

One of my most expensive investments paid off while preparing for Zepeda. My boxing gym hosted half of the training camp. Bobby went the extra mile and drove more than an hour several nights a week after coaching me in the morning.

Both of my trainers wouldn't be joining me for this fight. Julian reminded me that genuine relationships are deeper than a dollar sign. Julian's first fight with me would have been a career-changing payday, but he sacrificed the opportunity due to his loyalty and integrity.

He spent time training and building relationships with Jose Zepeda and me and didn't feel comfortable choosing a side. Most people would have played both sides of the fence and picked whichever side was most beneficial for them, but Julian is different from most people.

...

When I arrived in California, everyone noticed my calm demeanor during fight week. It came from the surety I felt and the confidence I built day-by-day and brick-by-brick. Each day was meaningful leading up to the event. Churchill hosted Monday's media workout and helped me feel at home in California.

Tuesday's media press conference made me reflect on my route to the top both times. I had professional boxing matches in rooms smaller than where my press conference was hosted inside the Hyatt Regency. Also, I was back headlining a card. Ironically, one of the first people to speak at the press conference was another two-time world champion.

Fernando Vargas has a larger-than-life persona, and his sons inherited that trait, which is essential for a boxing star. They were the first ones to take the stage at the press conference. It was inspirational to watch two generations of a boxing family. Their father said some gems that stuck with me.

I'm often asked about my kids becoming fighters, and like many other boxers, I don't aspire for my children to follow in my shoes as far as boxing is concerned. Everyone in boxing experiences the grueling grind, business, and politics of the sport. Only a few come out on top and most of the ones who do, wind up back at the bottom in worse conditions than when they started.

Nonetheless, why should we stop our kids from emulating us if it's naturally in them? A pro boxer knows best if another fighter has what it takes to become a successful boxer. Vargas saw that in his kids, so he decided to fully support them.

Boxing is a generational sport and like a fraternity. Most of the big names in boxing have ties to past generations of boxing or connections with people at the top. For the longest, I felt like I was on the outside looking in. I didn't feel a part of that fraternity in the boxing world until I became a world champion.

If my kids or nephews want to become pro boxers, they will take an entirely different path in the game than I did. The level of pressure will be higher due to the footsteps they are following, but they will have more resources than me when I began boxing.

Coming from a boxing family won't ensure a boxer's success, but becoming a fighter isn't the only career path in the sport. There are plenty of other careers, such as trainers, coaches, promoters, managers, and media. Our paths don't have to follow our predecessors, but it would be wise to leverage our predecessors' resources and connections.

My mind shifted from family to fighting again when Vargas proudly said that Mexican Americans are the best boxing fans in the world and that the arena would be packed with them on Saturday night. There was merit to Vargas's statement. I always knew that the Mexican American boxing fanbase is a passionate one. The fight between Mexican American boxing legends Fernando Vargas vs. Oscar De La Hoya was one of the most intense crowds I ever saw.

The first press conference of the week began making waves on social media and YouTube. Zepeda's team fussing with mine was just a preview of the audience action that upcoming Saturday. After the reporter on stage asked me a question, Evins started yelling what he had been saying the entire training camp. Evins barked, "This isn't a 50/50 fight!" across the room. During training camp, he would shout the same thing while pushing me to keep swimming or punching the bag when I was tired.

...

I know it's ironic for a Hurricane Katrina survivor to describe a special time in their life as the calm before the storm, but that was the only description of the energy in the air leading up to my fight against Zepeda. Thanksgiving and the World Cup dominated news headlines that week, but more attention began gravitating toward the fight once Friday rolled around. The laid-back hotel environment, which began feeling like an extended stay, was now hosting the weigh-ins. This was my time to rewrite history.

A storm led me to my calling, so I embrace all storms that come my way. There can't be a rainbow without rain. I know sunshine is on the other side of the storm, and there will be an opportunity to learn something valuable in the process. If I didn't experience the second storm in my career during boxing purgatory, who's to say that I would have reanalyzed my areas of improvement as meticulously as I did? I traveled through two storms in the boxing world. The first storm I endured was to get to the top, and the second was to reclaim my position.

I didn't realize I was fighting at 60% until my 27th fight. An experienced fighter will never be 100% injury-free because the rigors of boxing wouldn't allow it, but I was closer to 100% than I'd ever been. Boxing is old school in many of its values.

Current fighters are still doing most of the same training and boxing methods as pioneers of the sport. In comparison, most basketball players of previous eras weren't jumping out of the gym or shooting from almost half-court and football players weren't the physical specimens they are now. Boxing remains the purest to its creation.

Investing in a nutritionist revolutionized my game, but that resource isn't available to most boxers. Roughly two percent of professional boxers account for more than 90% of the revenue. Consequently, only a small percentage of pro fighters can afford a reputable nutritionist.

It's one thing to look better than you ever looked, but it's another thing to feel better than you ever felt also. The two rarely go hand-in-hand in boxing. Many boxers' bodies appear shredded at weigh-ins, but most are drained and miserable at that time because they had to dehydrate and starve their body to make the necessary weight to fight and not get fined or have their bout canceled.

I'd been drinking two gallons of water and eating two small meals a day with minimal carbs for two weeks leading up to the fight. On Thanksgiving night, my team and I walked down the street to another hotel to lose the last six pounds before weigh-ins on Friday morning.

When we got to the room, I took a hot bath for thirty minutes. Then I was wrapped in 15+ bath towels while I laid on the bed and sweated out the two gallons of water per day I had been drinking over the past few weeks. While I was stretched out on the bed looking like a plus-sized mummy, my wife and I passionately debated world views while the team laughed and shared their stances. Then I returned to the tub, where I started another round of bathing and watching a documentary.

The debates, jokes, laughs, and entertainment sped up the methodical process of losing two pounds an hour. I walked into the hotel room weighing 146 pounds and left out 140. It felt like a cruel trick that I had to do all this on Thanksgiving night while most of the country was enjoying their favorite meals of the year. However, that was a minimal sacrifice compared to the countless number of other sacrifices I made to get here. I was hours away from all the sacrifices, including bus rides to the gym, moving away from home, 15+ years of hard work, and rivers of blood, sweat, and tears potentially paying off.

The sacrifice of giving each day my all alleviated the pressure before the fight. I had been here before. I knew what it took to get here and did even more the second time around. My opponent knew what it took to get here, but he never made it through a storm before. The storm prepared me for the opportunity to shine forever.

My family, friends, and fans believed in
me, but no one believed in my
vision more than I did.

————————

LESSON

CHAPTER 32

War Grounds

From the outside looking in, I was in a pressure-filled situation. I was a few months away from my 34th birthday, overlooked and ducked my entire career, and facing a fight that would be the start of a blissful beginning or a return flight to boxing purgatory.

I never asked myself questions naysayers asked, such as, "What would happen if I lost?" or "What would happen if I underperformed?" My work ethic and learning experiences erased the what-ifs and uncertainty.

Zepeda and I were two fighters entering our primes, ranked at the top of the division, and fighting for a world title. There are levels to boxing and levels to motivation. Thinking about what was on the other side of this battle ignited my soul to get everything I came for.

It had been unusually cold in LA during fight week until Saturday, the day I would have to fight outside. The fight was in Carson, California, at The Health Dignity System, better known as the War Grounds. It was warm during the day, but as the afternoon turned into the evening, it began getting cold again.

The calmness escaped my body gradually as fight day progressed. I woke up with it on my mind and knew what time it was once I opened my eyes. It was a relief to eat a meal shortly after I woke up. I couldn't define what I was experiencing at the time, but Declan knew I slipped into a different mode when he brought me my breakfast the morning of the fight. The build-up of staying in a hotel all week, waiting three years for this moment, and busting my ass for over a decade began boiling over.

My leg tapped like a sewing machine on the coffee table as my team and I waited in my room to depart for the War Grounds at 5:00 PM. Most of the words around me sounded like background noise. While my team and I piled into the Mercedes Sprinter, I thought about the days of driving to my own fights and fighting for free. Now, my team and I were being driven in a six-figure vehicle to earn seven figures for a fight. As good as the money may sound, that was the last thing on my mind.

Putting my hands on Zepeda was the first thing on my mind when I exited the Sprinter after we arrived at the arena. My opponent had to pay for all the hard work I had been putting in and standing in my way to make history. Once we were settled into the locker room, the energy in the room differed from a stereotypical boxing locker room before a fight. We calmly watched the preliminary bouts leading up to the main event. No music was playing until Hollywood began playing Lil Wayne on his phone.

Jermall Charlo brought some magnetic energy into the locker room 30 minutes after we were settled in. He greeted my entire team with warm gestures, and then pumped some motivation into my veins. I was less than an hour away from potentially joining him, his brother, and Errol Spence Jr. again as world champions fighting out of Texas.

Several months earlier, Jermell made history by becoming the undisputed champion of the 154-pound division in the same arena. We came a long way from catching the bus and being overlooked together in the trenches. While I loosened my shoulders and bounced around shadowboxing, Jermall shouted, "Take his heart Regis! Take his heart Regis!" Charlo's message and presence were perfect, like the rest of my week and preparation during training camp.

Moments later, we got word that we would be walking to the ring in five minutes. The atmosphere in the locker room was like a group of soldiers entering enemy territory to take over their turf. That five minutes flew by, and it was go-time before I knew it. The energy we spent cultivating during training camp was now surfacing in the locker room before it was time for the ring walk.

One of the most distinct details about moments is the energy captured in them. Once my professional career started taking off, I hired cameraman, Mike De Leon, to begin documenting film of my day-to-day life and other special moments of my career. Most of my time in boxing purgatory was spent in my gym training. While not knowing my next move, I applied the pain of uncertainty to my grind.

My wife was locked in on the fitness grind with me throughout that timeframe. Her presence next to me in our gym during one of the darkest times in my career gave me an extra wave of energy. We evolved to new levels physically and developed a routine of playing music while working out together or with Evins. After Raquel wrapped up her workout, she began filming me exercise. Once the camera began rolling, Meek Mill's track, "Wins & Losses," featuring Eric Thomas, came on.

While going the extra mile, I often think about how few people are traveling with me. As I began getting deeper into my bag working out, Eric Thomas passionately came on the track and said, "You have to eat the dream. You have to sleep the dream. You have to dream the dream. You have to see it when nobody else sees it. You have to feel it when it's not tangible. You have to believe it when you cannot see it. You have to be possessed with the dream." At that moment, I was ready to fight my next opponent.

My grind epitomized his motivational speech. Morning, afternoon, evening, and night, I was grinding to get my belt back. I was on the outside looking in and didn't have a title fight in sight. No one expected me to be in the mix for a belt at the time, but I knew I would become a 2x world champion someway, somehow. I didn't have a belt in my possession, but I kept imagining one wrapped around my shoulders. My family, friends, and fans believed in me, but no one believed in my vision more than I did.

I visualized the opportunity to become a world champion again so many times that I wasn't surprised when the moment came. Many songs crossed my mind for the ring walk, but none was more fitting than the one that captured my energy and mindset while I was in boxing purgatory.

The walk that used to seem so long was a quick path to the ring. I heard the boos before I showed my face to the crowd. Once I exited the curtains, a smile emerged on my face. The Mexican American crowd that Fernando Vargas spoke of was booing in my direction as if their hate for me would help their beloved fighter in a ring where no one else could help him.

Most of the crowd harmonized with the Mexican national anthem. A man representing two countries felt double the amount of pressure. It may have been triple the pressure for him because this was his third time fighting for a world title. Superstitions sometimes trick us out of our position. The saying, "Third time is the charm," held no weight.

If Zepeda lost, he would have a harder time getting another title shot than me because he hadn't been a world champion yet. I felt that he was one of the best boxers in the sport who hadn't become a world champion. When I stared across the ring, I knew he was ready for war and to lay it all on the line against me.

I was in control of the fight from the opening round, but every now and then, Zepeda landed a punch that gave his fanbase hope he could pull off an upset. Both of us were cut early into the fight.

A cut man is one of the most underrated roles in boxing. It's like an insurance policy that will save your ass when you need it, but you don't want to have to use it. Aaron, my cut man, was busy at the end of the second round.

Zepeda and I began shedding blood during the early rounds. There have been plenty of fighters who weren't hurt but lost because of mismanaged cuts and swelling. I was thankful to have Aaron on my team.

Being a conscious fighter is an overlooked quality. I felt that I was up on the cards during the mid-rounds, but you can never be too sure when you are fighting on someone else's turf. After the 7th round, I asked Bobby if I was up on the cards. He fills the role of a general by knowing what to tell his soldier in the midst of a war and in between rounds.

During a fight with another one of his boxers, the power went out in the arena after the 11th round. He was on the verge of being knocked out and had already been knocked down several times during the fight, but Bobby told him what he needed to hear during the unexpected intermission.

When the stadium lights came back on, the nearly defeated fighter's lights came back on, also. Bobby's help led him to victory. I didn't need an unnatural act to happen, but Bobby's reminder that we didn't need to leave it up to the judges made me turn it up a notch. At the same time heading into the 8th round, Zepeda's corner told him he was up on the cards.

I took in that moment alone, but having
my team, family, and friends at the top
with me meant the world.

———————

LESSON

CHAPTER 33

Championship Rounds

C hampionship rounds are given that title for a reason. These intense closing moments boil down to who wants it more, who is in better shape, and who will do what it takes to come out on top.

Experience comes in many forms and fashions. I knew what it was like to fight uptight. The pressure from my first major boxing match in New Orleans made me tense. Consequently, it was hard to find my rhythm. Finding your rhythm while being tense is counterproductive. Zepeda had difficulty finding his rhythm and fought straight up with his hands down most of the night.

During the 10th round, he brought the fight the fans wanted to see. He lured me into exchanging combinations with him. Before that round, he avoided major damage by leaning away from my punches and throwing a punch, then getting out of the way. Halfway into the 10th round, my jaw met his left hand. It snapped my head back, but his best shot of the night did me a favor.

That punch would have knocked out most fighters, but I spit it out and returned fire that sent him against the ropes. He fought back, and the crowd roared in his favor, but he was back in survival mode.

That punch would have taken my legs if I weren't in great shape. I trained like a champion so I could perform like one when it mattered the most. The championship rounds are the deep end, and that's where I wanted to take him.

I live in the deep end and feel most alive when I'm most at risk. I had cuts and bruises, sustained powerful punches, and moved fluidly for ten rounds, but I had enough energy to go for several more rounds. Nonetheless, I was in the midst of being tested.

Toward the later rounds, I began to see my opponent and his fans tiring. When the bell for the 11th round rang, Charlo's message before the fight, "Take his heart," replayed in my head.

Zepeda earned a new level of respect from me during our fight. He fought through shots that would have dropped other opponents and made me feel his power. A fighting chance was the last thing I wanted to give him.

During the end of the 10th round was the first time I knew he was hurt. He fought cautiously to start the 11th round, and I knew I had to go with my move. I began walking him down and looking for my opening.

The flow state is one of the best states to be in when creating something, whether it's a book or a moment in history. A moment in history was created when a left hand that Zepeda had been trying to avoid for 30+ minutes connected square on his right cheek. The punch snapped Zepeda's head back and made the crowd roar.

I followed up with several punches after the left overhand, so I didn't know which punch it was at the time that put my opponent on his last leg. The combination sent him against the ropes, but we didn't stay there long. Moments after I landed another flurry of punches, Zepeda slid down the ropes onto the canvas. The ref waved off the fight before he could count to three.

I released the pain from my soul into the atmosphere of the War Grounds after making history and stopping my opponent in the 11th round. While adrenaline pumped through my veins, I flexed my newly ripped frame, drenched in blood and sweat, to reclaim my spot at the top of my division.

After winning, ring personnel guided me to a neutral corner by myself. I took in that moment alone, but having my team, family, and friends at the top with me meant the world. Zepeda's fans supported him during the defeat by booing me. I watched one of them give me the middle finger, but chants of my name drowned out the hate. Boos from the other side didn't last long because they received their money's worth, and their fighter showed a ton of heart.

Leading up to the fight, I imagined plenty of different outcomes. I visualized an early or mid-round knockout and going the distance without getting touched. The outcome was unexpected.

Before the post-fight interview in the ring, I knew I had just fought one of my toughest opponents thus far. Overcoming what he brought to the table made my victory even more gratifying. I didn't beat a scrub to become a champion. I beat a man who has the ability to become a world champion. It just wasn't his time.

It's easy to only think about yourself while accomplishing one of your biggest goals. Bobby and I thought about more than ourselves after the victory. He was one of the first people to help my opponent up after the fight ended.

Shortly after getting the microphone in the ring, I gave Zepeda props and encouraged him to keep striving to become a world champion. He deserved to share the moment with me. Good karma paid off from the sportsmanship I showed in the past. He was respectful in defeat, which speaks volumes about his character.

During previous post-fight interviews, I used to call out other fighters. My accomplishment of becoming a two-time world champion ended those days. Now, they would have to say my name.

To be continued.